# PLAYBOY'S PARTY JOKES

Selected by the editors of PLAYBOY Magazine

Femlin illustrations by LeRoy Neiman

**A PLAYBOY POCKET BOOK**

The hungover couple dawdled over a mid-afternoon breakfast, after a particularly wild all-night party held in their fashionable apartment.

"Dearest, this is rather embarrassing," said the husband, "but was it you I made love to in the library last night?"

His wife looked at him reflectively, and then asked, "About what time?"

A friend of ours reports that during a recent drive down to Miami Beach he spotted a sign near a real-estate development that read: GET LOTS WHILE YOU'RE YOUNG.

"Anything else, sir?" asked the attentive bellhop, trying his best to make the lady and gentleman comfortable in their penthouse suite in the posh hotel.

"No. No, thank you," replied the gentleman.

"Anything for your wife, sir?" the bellhop asked.

"Why, yes, young man," said the gentleman. "Would you bring me a postcard?"

Everyone in the smart night club was amazed by the old gentleman, obviously pushing 70, tossing off manhattans and cavorting around the dance floor like a 20-year-old. Finally, curiosity got the best of the cigarette girl.

"I beg your pardon, sir," she said, "but I'm amazed to see a gentleman of your age living it up like a youngster. Tell me, are all of your faculties unimpaired?"

The old fellow looked up at the girl sadly and shook his head. "Not all, I'm afraid," he said. "Just last evening I went night-clubbing with a girlfriend—we drank and danced all night and finally rolled into her place about two A.M. We went to bed immediately and I was asleep almost as soon as my head hit the pillow. I woke around 3:30 and nudged my girl. 'Why, George,' she said in surprise, 'we did that just 15 minutes ago.'

"So you see," the old boy said sadly, "my memory is beginning to fail me."

We just learned that one of the showgirls from the Latin Quarter disappeared last week and hasn't been obscene since.

Our Unabashed Dictionary defines a *bachelor* as a man who has no children, to speak of.

"Why did you spend so much time parked in that fellow's automobile last night?" demanded the irate mother. "I could hear the giggling and squealing for a

4

"Of _course_ there's someone else!"

good half-hour."

"But, Mom," answered her daughter, "if a fellow takes you to the movies you ought to at *least* kiss him goodnight."

"I thought you went to the Stork Club?" countered the mother.

"We did."

**O**ur Unabashed Dictionary defines *chaperone* as one who could never make the team, but is still in there intercepting passes.

**"Y**ou know," said the gossip-loving office cutie to her lunch companion, "I'd *never* say anything about Margaret unless I could say something good. And, sister, is this *good* . . ."

**"I**'m looking for adventure, excitement, beautiful women," cried the young man to his father as he prepared to leave home. "Don't try to stop me, I'm on my way."

"Who's trying to stop you?" shouted his father. "Take me along."

**W**e know a real friendly hatcheck girl who thinks that strip poker is a swell game because the fellows always give back her clothes.

**O**ur tireless Research Department, after extensive house-to-house canvassing, has come up with the three

*"Sedgewick, will you <u>please</u> go to sleep?"*

best things in life: a martini before and a nap after.

**A**fter gunning his Mercedes the wrong way down a one-way street, the rather inebriated young man was asked where he thought he was going by an inquisitive police officer.

"I'm not really sure," confessed the drunk, "but wherever it is, I must be late, because everybody seems to be coming back already."

**T**he none-too-bright young fellow had been dating the same girl for more than a year and one evening the girl's father confronted him and wanted to know whether the lad's intentions toward his daughter were honorable or dishonorable.

"Gee," said the young man, swallowing hard, "I didn't know I had a choice!"

**A** distinguished Shakespearean actor and an eminent English drama critic were lunching together in a London club when the conversation, as usual, turned to the Bard.

"Tell me," asked the critic of the actor, "is it your opinion that Shakespeare intended us to believe Hamlet had sexual relations with Ophelia?"

"I don't know what Shakespeare intended," said the actor, "but I usually do."

During a grouse hunt in North Carolina two intrepid sportsmen were blasting away at a clump of trees near a stone wall. Suddenly a red-faced country squire popped his head over the wall and shouted, "Hey, you almost hit my wife."

"Did I?" cried the hunter, aghast. "Terribly sorry. Have a shot at mine over there."

We enjoyed a luncheon date the other day with a lovely Broadway showgirl who confessed she was unsuccessful in show business until she had her "*no's*" fixed.

Pouring out his troubles to his great and good friend over a couple of triple martinis, Brad had to confess that things weren't going too well at home.

"My wife and I just don't hit it off at night," he was saying to Bart. "I hate to admit it, but I'm afraid I just don't know how to make her happy."

"Hell, boy," said Bart, "there's really nothing to it. Let me give you some advice. At bedtime, switch on a new Sinatra platter, turn all the lights low and spray some perfume around the room. Next, tell your wife to get into her sheerest nightie; then make sure you raise the bottom window."

"Then what do I do?" asked Brad.

"Just whistle."

"Whistle?"

"That's right. I'll be waiting outside the window. When I hear you whistle, I'll come right up and finish the job."


The naive miss was seated in her doctor's office.

"Our tests indicate that you are pregnant," said the M.D., "and there is every indication that you are going to have twins."

"But how can that be, Doctor?" the girl protested. "I've never been out on a double date in my life."


The wealthy old gentleman and his wife were celebrating their 35th wedding anniversary and their three grown sons joined them for dinner. The old man was rather irritated when he discovered that none of the

*"I'll drink to that!"*

boys had bothered to bring a gift and after the meal, he drew them aside.

"You're all grown men," he said, "and old enough to hear this. Your mother and I have never been legally married."

"What?" gasped one of the sons. "Do you mean to say we're all bastards?"

"Yes," snapped the old man, "and cheap ones, too."

A most attractive redhead, window-shopping on Fifth Avenue, became aware of a well-dressed gentleman following her at a short distance. Somewhat flustered, she accidentally dropped her handbag and he immediately retrieved it for her.

"I dropped that bag accidentally," she said. "I want you to understand that I am not the type of girl you can pick up."

The gentleman smiled and said, "Madam, I am most assuredly not picking you up. I am picking you out."

A cute young secretary we know enjoys telling everyone that her boss takes great pleasure in grabbing her by the knee. "But yesterday," she cooed at us over dry martinis, "he reached a new high."

The father, passing through his son's college town late one evening on a business trip, thought he would pay his boy a surprise visit. Arriving at the lad's fraternity house, dad rapped loudly on the door. After several

"Sometimes I think I'd like to move to another
city and start all over as a virgin."

minutes of knocking, a sleepy voice drifted down from a second-floor window, "Waddyah want?"

"Does Ramsey Duncan live here?" asked the father.

"Yeah," replied the voice. "Dump him on the front porch."

**"H**ow did you spend the weekend?" asked the pretty brunette secretary of her blonde companion.

"Fishing through the ice," she said.

"Fishing through the ice? Whatever for?"

"Olives."

**"D**o you cheat on your wife?" asked the psychiatrist.

"Who else?" answered the patient.

**O**ur Unabashed Dictionary defines *bachelor* as a fellow who is crazy to get married—and knows it.

**O**ne steno observed to another, as the boss' sexy secretary wiggled past the water cooler: "There goes the original good time that was had by all."

The sweet young thing was telling her mother about the great time she had at the mountain resort: "I met a man in the recreation hall and we played Ping-Pong all afternoon. What fun, Mother!"

"Why, dear," remarked the mother, "I never knew you enjoyed Ping-Pong."

"I do now," the daughter said. "I'd hit the ball the wrong way and we'd both go after it under the table. Then he'd hit the ball the wrong way and we'd both go after it under the table. We played all afternoon. It was wonderful."

"But I don't understand," said the mother. "Where does the fun come in?"

"Under the table, silly."

While visiting our country, a lovely French maiden found herself out of money just as her visa expired.

Unable to pay her passage back to France, she was in despair until an enterprising sailor made her a sporting proposition. "My ship is sailing tonight," he said. "I'll smuggle you aboard, hide you down in the hold and provide you with a mattress, blankets and food. All it will cost you is a little love."

The girl consented and late that night the sailor snuck her on board his vessel. Twice each day, thereafter, the sailor smuggled a large tray of food below decks, took his pleasure with the little French stowaway and departed. The days turned into weeks and the weeks might have turned into months, if the captain hadn't noticed the sailor carrying food below one evening and followed him. After witnessing this unique bit of barter, he waited until the sailor had departed and then confronted the girl, demanding an explanation. She told him the whole story. "Hmm," mused the captain. "A clever arrangement, and I must say I admire that young seaman's ingenuity. However, Miss, I feel it is only fair to tell you that this is the Staten Island Ferry."

A psychologist is a man who watches everybody else when a beautiful girl enters the room.

His lion trainer had quit without notice and the circus manager needed someone to replace him for the next night's show. He put an ad in the local paper and the next morning two applicants showed up outside his office. One was a rather ordinary-looking young man

*"The bartender's my husband."*

and the other a ravishing, redheaded beauty. Neither one of them looked very much like a lion trainer, but the manager was desperate.

"All right," he said, "here's a whip, and a chair and a gun. Let's see what you can do with Big Leo over there. We'll let you have the first try, miss, but be careful—he's a mean one."

The ravishing redhead strode past the whip, and the chair, and the gun, and empty-handed, fearlessly entered the cage.

Big Leo rose, snarling, then came charging across the cage toward her with a ferocious roar. When the lion was almost upon her, the girl threw open her coat. Underneath, she was stark naked. Leo skidded to a stop and crawled the rest of the way on his belly; he nuzzled the girl's feet with his nose, purred and licked her trim ankles.

The astonished circus manager grinned happily and turned to the popeyed young man. "Well, young fella," he asked, "think you can top *that*?"

"Yeah," breathed the man. "Just get that stupid lion out of there."

A bachelor is a man who believes in life, liberty and the happiness of pursuit.

Our Unabashed Dictionary defines *nice girl* as one who whispers sweet nothing-doings in your ear.

The husband who knows where his wife keeps her

"Miss Watkins, may I have the very great pleasure of taking you to the club's New Year's Eve dance?"

nickels and dimes has nothing on the husband who knows where to find the maid's quarters.

We suppose you've heard about the man on the flying trapeze who caught his wife in the act.

Coming home unexpectedly, the husband found his wife in bed with a naked man. He produced a pistol from a dresser drawer and was about to shoot the interloper when his wife pleaded, "Don't, don't! Who do you think bought us that house in the country, that beautiful Cadillac, my sable wrap?"

"Are *you* the man?" asked the husband. The unclothed one nodded. "Then get your clothes on," roared the husband, "you wanna catch cold?"

Then there was the professional lady who bought a bicycle and peddled it all over town.

The rural lady had been coming into the city hospital regularly to give birth to her annual child. When she was packing up to go home after her 10th trip, the nurse said, "Well, Mrs. Slocum, I suppose we'll be seeing you again next year, as usual?"

"No, ma'am," drawled Mrs. Slocum. "My husband and I jest found out what's been causin' it."

The girl sitting daintily on the bar stool was luscious, shapely and tempting. Naturally, she aroused the interest of the playboy at the other end of the bar. He smiled at her. Then he winked. When this failed, he tried out his best leer. Just then the bartender—200 pounds of muscle with a hairy chest—leaned over the bar and said, "Look, Buster, that there's my wife. So cut the funny business, understand?"

Replied the flustered playboy, "Funny business? I don't know what you're talking about. I just dropped in for a cool drink. Give me a piece of beer."

An interloper at a meeting of the Society of Mayflower Descendants put the august group in a bit of a tizzy when he responded, "Actually, I'm descended from a long line my mother once heard."

A recently deposed Eastern potentate (who shall remain unnamed) was known for his prowess in the harem—often entertaining no less than a dozen wives per night. Shorn of his crown and possessions, he was seeking employment and was overjoyed when an

American theatrical agent signed him up to perform these same feats at certain choice and private showings. The contract was signed, bookings were scheduled and 12 delectable beauties hired for the premiere. The box office was sold out. The audience waited eagerly, for they had paid $10 per ticket to see the fabulous potentate. A symphony orchestra struck up an overture, the lights dimmed, the curtains parted and the dozen lovelies were revealed, reclining on couches. The potentate stepped briskly out from the wings, bowed to the audience, then proceeded. Naturally, after such a build-up, the audience was disappointed when the great man fell flat on his face after taking pleasure with only four of the beauties. They howled for their money back, and the theatrical agent regretfully had to comply. Later he went backstage and wailed to the potentate, "I'm ruined! How could you do this to me? What happened?"

The potentate shook his head sadly. "I don't understand it," he said. "Everything went smoothly this afternoon at dress rehearsal."

The young Georgia miss came to the hospital for a checkup.

"Have you been X-rayed?" asked the doctor.

"Nope," she said, "but ah've been ultraviolated."

The doctor had just finished giving the young man a thorough physical examination.

"The best thing for you to do," the M.D. said, "is

22

"As a kid star in pictures . . . you've had it."

give up drinking and smoking, get to bed early and stay away from women."

"Doc, I don't deserve the best," said the patient. "What's next best?"

Three playboys—English, Arabian and American—were standing on a street corner in Casablanca when a spectacular Oriental beauty walked haughtily by them. "By Jove!" exclaimed the Englishman. "By Allah!" sighed the Arabian. "By tomorrow night," said the American.

After a particularly tiring performance, a beautiful New York showgirl returned to her apartment and found a half-dozen handsome admirers waiting there, with nought on their minds but amour. "How sweet of you boys to surprise me like this," she cooed, "but, really, I've had an awfully tough show tonight and I'm simply exhausted. I'm afraid one or two of you will have to go home."

A little girl answered the knock on the door of the farmhouse. The caller, a rather troubled-looking, middle-aged man, asked to see her father.

"If you've come about the bull," she said, "he's $50. We have the papers and everything and he's guaranteed."

"Young lady," the man said, "I want to see your father."

"If that's too much," the little girl replied, "we got

"I'll be out with Miss Marlow all evening,
Thomas. Have the iron lung ready
when I get back."

another bull for $25, and he's guaranteed, too, but he doesn't have any papers."

"Young lady," the man repeated, "I want to see your father!"

"If that's too much," said the little girl, "we got another bull for only $10, but he's not guaranteed."

"I'm not here for a bull," said the man angrily. "I want to talk about your brother, Elmer. He's gotten my daughter in trouble!"

"Oh, I'm sorry," said the little girl. "You'll have to see Pa about that, 'cause I don't know what he charges for Elmer."

"I'm sorry, George," she said, "I can never learn to love you."

"Gee, that's too bad," said George, "and after I'd saved nearly 10 grand, too."

"Give me one more lesson."

"To me," said one, "he's a pain in the neck."

"Strange," said the other, "I had a much lower opinion of him."

He asked her for a burning kiss;
She said in accents cruel,
"I may be quite a red-hot gal,
But I'm nobody's fuel."

Gina Lottabazooma, the shapely Italian screen siren, was put under contract by a Hollywood studio and brought to the U.S. to make an epic Western.

"I absolutely refuse to play this scene," she exclaimed.

"But, Gina," explained the director, "all you have to do is point out the direction the outlaws took when the sheriff and his posse ride up to you."

"I know," said the star, "but have you read the screen action in the script?"

"What do you mean?"

"Look how I'm supposed to point," snapped the star. "It says here that I am to place both hands behind my back, take a deep breath, turn north and say, 'They went thataway!' "

The young man was determined to win his girl that evening.

"I have loved you more than you will ever know," he said.

"So I was right," she exclaimed, slapping him across the face. "You *did* take advantage of me last

Saturday night when I was drunk!"

**T**he husband came strolling in the front door to discover his wife in the passionate embrace of his best friend.

"I love him, John," she said to her surprised spouse.

"See here," said the friend, "we're all too sophisticated to let a situation like this get out of hand. Tell you what let's do—we're both sportsmen—I'll play you a game of gin rummy for her."

The husband thought about that for a moment.

"All right," he said, "but let's play for a penny-a-point on the side, just to keep it interesting."

**A** young bride's mother was helping unpack after the honeymoon and was shocked to find her daughter's trousseau badly torn.

"Darling," she gasped, "didn't your husband like your trousseau?"

"Oh, yes," the blushing bride replied, "he liked my trousseau, mother. It's just that he liked my torso more than my trousseau—that's why my trousseau is tore so."

**T**he young reporter was interviewing a woman who had just reached her 100th birthday.

"To what do you attribute your remarkable good health?" he asked.

"Well," she said thoughtfully, "I've always eaten moderately, worked hard, I don't smoke or drink, and

*"They don't seem to have one for that."*

I keep good hours."

"Have you ever been bedridden?" the reporter asked.

"Well, sure," said the elderly lady, "but don't put that in your paper."


This is old, but it has always been one of our favorites.

The young playboy took a blind date to an amusement park. They went for a ride on the Ferris wheel. The ride completed, she seemed rather bored.

"What would you like to do next?" he asked.

"I wanna be weighed," she said. So the young man took her over to the weight guesser. "112," said the man at the scale, and he was absolutely right.

Next they rode the roller coaster. After that, he bought her some popcorn and cotton candy, then he asked what else she would like to do.

"I wanna be weighed," she said.

I really latched onto a square one tonight, thought the young man, and using the excuse that he had developed a headache, he took the girl home.

The girl's mother was surprised to see her home so early, and asked, "What's wrong, dear, didn't you have a nice time tonight?"

"Wousy," said the girl.


The husband wired home that he had been able to wind up his business trip a day early and would be home on Thursday. When he walked into his apartment, however, he found his wife in bed with another

*"That, you might say, has been the story of Ralph's life."*

man. Furious, he picked up his bag and stormed out; he met his mother-in-law on the street, told her what had happened and announced that he was filing suit for divorce in the morning.

"Give my daughter a chance to explain before you take any action," the older woman pleaded. Reluctantly, he agreed.

An hour later, his mother-in-law phoned the husband at his club.

"I knew my daughter would have an explanation," she said, a note of triumph in her voice. "She didn't receive your telegram!"


"Your Honor," said the husband suing for divorce, "my wife beats me."

"And just how often does she beat you?" queried the judge.

"She beats me every time, Your Honor."

The mother entered the darkened room unexpectedly

and found daughter and boyfriend in passionate embrace on the sofa.

"Well—I never!" exclaimed mother.

"But, mother, you must have!" said daughter.

A girl's conscience doesn't really keep her from doing anything wrong—it merely keeps her from enjoying it.

We know a modern Cinderella who, at the stroke of midnight, turns into a motel.

At breakfast one morning Lady Cribblesfram suggested to His Lordship that since their son, Reginald, was fast approaching manhood, someone should be telling him "about the birds and bees."

Lord Cribblesfram did not welcome discussion on matters so delicate, but he recognized a father's duty and so, that evening after dinner, he summoned his son to his study.

"Er . . . ahem . . . Reginald," he began uneasily, "Lady Cribblesfram and I both feel it is time you and I had a man-to-man talk on the subject of . . . uh . . . the birds and bees."

"Yes, Pater," said Reginald brightly.

"Son, do you remember our trip to Paris last summer?"

"Yes, sir."

"And do you remember our visit to the Folies-Bergère?"

"I do, Pater."

"You will then, perhaps, remember our drinking with the two lovely ladies from the Folies?"

"I do, indeed, Pater."

"And afterward, you remember our taking them to our hotel and what we did there?"

"Yes, sir."

"Well, son," said Lord Cribblesfram, wiping the perspiration from his brow, "it's very much like that with the birds and bees, too."

Paul Revere's horse galloped down the country road. The life of the colonies depended on his warning the people that the British were coming. He approached a farmhouse.

"Is your husband at home?" he called to the woman feeding chickens in the yard.

"He's back in the barn, Paul," she answered.

"Tell him to get his musket and go to the village square. The Redcoats are coming!"

The exchange of words had taken but an instant;

*"But suppose we had a short guest?"*

Revere's horse had not broken its stride. The famous patriot thundered off toward the next farm.

"Is your husband at home?" Revere called to the woman in the doorway of the next farmhouse he approached.

"He's asleep in his room, Paul," she said.

"Tell him to get on his clothes," Revere cried. "The Minute Men are meeting at the village square. The British are coming!"

Horse and rider galloped on to still another home.

"Is your husband at home?" he called to the handsome woman who leaned out the window.

"He's gone to New Amsterdam and won't be back till Sunday," she said.

"Whoa-a-a!"

A cool friend informs us that the best way to cut off a cat's tail is to repossess his Jaguar.

One of the airlines recently introduced a special half-fare rate for wives accompanying their husbands on business trips. Anticipating some valuable testimonials, the publicity department of the airline sent out letters to all the wives of businessmen who used the special rates, asking how they enjoyed their trip.

Responses are still pouring in asking, "What trip?"

An attractive, but not-too-bright girl of our acquaintance nearly ruined herself before discovering that what the doctor ordered was not, as she misunderstood,

*"But, sir—it is his last request . . ."*

"three hearty males a day."

A flashy Mercedes-Benz roared up to the curb, where a cute young miss stood waiting for a taxi.

"Hi," said the gentleman at the wheel. "I'm going west."

"How wonderful," came the cool reply. "Bring me back an orange."

"I notice your daughter didn't get home until three o'clock this morning," said Mrs. Tyson to Mrs. Frisbee across the backyard fence. "*My* daughter was in the house before midnight."

"I know," answered Mrs. Frisbee coolly. "But, you see, my daughter walked home."

A socially prominent dowager from Boston was visiting friends in New York and a dinner party was held in her honor. She was seated next to another younger woman, and began discussing the relative merits of

Boston society.

"In Boston," she said, "we place all our emphasis on good breeding."

"In New York we think it's a lot of fun, too," agreed the other woman, "but we also manage to foster other interests."


"Your wife will probably hit the ceiling when you get home tonight," said the barfly to his drinking companion.

"Yeah," said the companion. "She's a lousy shot!"


The farmer had borrowed a bull from a neighbor to service his two cows. He put the beast in the pasture and instructed his son to keep an eye on them. "As soon as the bull has finished, you come up to the house and tell me," he said.

When the farmer got back to the house, he found the Reverend there paying a social call. They were seated in the front room sipping tea when the boy burst in the door.

"Dad, Dad," he exclaimed, "the bull just — — — — — the brown cow!"

Greatly embarrassed, the farmer took his son outside. "Is that any way to talk in front of the Reverend?" he demanded. "Why couldn't you have said the bull '*surprised*' the brown cow? I would've understood. Now go back down to the pasture and come tell me when the bull is finished."

A few minutes later the boy again burst into the

room.

"Dad, Dad——" he exclaimed.

Fearing another breach of verbal etiquette, the father interrupted.

"I know, I know," he said. "The bull has *surprised* the white cow."

"He sure has," exclaimed the excited boy. "He — — — — — the brown cow again!"


One of the members of the smart cabana club asked the lifeguard how he might teach a young lady of his acquaintance to swim.

"It takes considerable time and technique," the lifeguard said. "First you must take her into the water. Then place one arm about her waist, hold her tightly, then take her right arm and raise it slowly . . ."

"This certainly will be helpful," said the member, "and I know my sister will appreciate it."

"Your sister?" said the lifeguard. "In that case, just push her off the end of the pier."


"Darling," he breathed, "after making love I doubt if I'll ever be able to get over you—so would you mind answering the phone?"


Two inebriated gentlemen stood at the bar near closing time.

"I've an idea," said one, "lesh have one more drink and then go find us shum girls."

"Naw," replied the other. "I've got more than I

*"What! I need exercise?!"*

can handle at home."

"Great," replied the idea man, "then lesh have one more drink and go up to your place."


**T**hey hadn't seen their friend in nearly five years—not since he received a movie contract and went to Hollywood. Now he was back visiting in the Midwestern town where he had lived as a boy.

His friends were pleased to see him and anxious to learn if all the wild stories they had heard about life in Hollywood were really true.

"Nonsense," said the film celebrity. "Hollywood is no different than any other American city. Life out there is normal and well-ordered: a movie actress isn't very different from a working housewife in Minneapolis or Milwaukee; a movie director is no more eccentric than the office manager of one of the businesses right here.

"Take my own case: I'm up early every morning, at the studio by 8:15; I work a full, hard day and I'm home every evening by six; dinner, afterward the evening paper, and I'm into bed before 10.

"Why just the other day, I was saying to my wife: 'George . . .'"


**T**he passionate young thing was having a difficult time getting across what she wanted from her rather dense boyfriend. Finally, she asked, "Would you like to see where I was operated on for appendicitis?"

"Gosh, no!" he replied. "I hate hospitals."

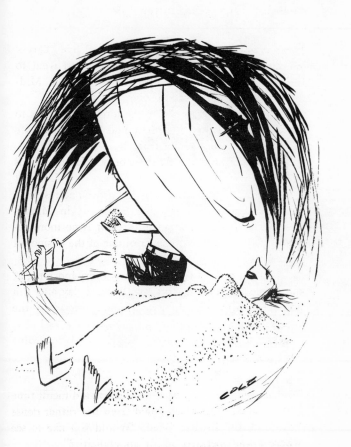

You've undoubtedly heard about the top-salaried movie director who was always trying to make a little extra.

A spinster schoolteacher took her fifth-grade charges on a field trip to a county fair. There was a race track on the grounds and she asked them whether they would enjoy seeing the horses. The children enthusiastically exclaimed they would, but as soon as she got them inside the gate, they all requested to be taken to the lavatory. She accompanied the little girls, but sent the boys to the men's room alone. They trooped out almost immediately and announced that the facilities were too high for them to reach.

The situation was an awkward one, but after looking about to make sure she was unobserved, the teacher ushered the boys back in. She lined them up before the plumbing and moved methodically down the line. After lifting several, she came to one who was unusually heavy.

"Goodness," she exclaimed, "are you in the fifth?"

"Hell no, lady," came the startled reply. "I'm riding Blue Grass in the third."

Lord Cramsfedder was startled out of his sleep by his trusted valet, Gordon.

"Oh, M'lord, there's a bounder in congress with Her Ladyship," announced the servant.

Lord Cramsfedder leaped out of his bed, hastily slipped into his robe and grabbed his fowling piece from the mantle. Together they proceeded upstairs on tiptoes, and cautiously pushed open the door to Her Ladyship's boudoir. The situation was immediately obvious. The outraged husband lifted the weapon, aimed carefully, and blasted away with both barrels.

When the smoke had cleared, Gordon looked in. "Oh, sir," he cried out, his voice filled with admiration, "a sportsman ever, you got him on the rise."

News item: Mrs. Bradley Fowler was granted a divorce after she told the judge her husband had spoken to her only three times since they were married. Mrs. Fowler was awarded the custody of their three children.

We've just received this tidbit from a usually reliable source concerning a certain Senator who, it seems, had to visit Chicago recently for a Committee Hearing and wanted to take a female acquaintance along.

"I have Senatorial immunity," he assured her, "so you needn't be afraid of the Mann Act."

"Afraid of it?" she giggled. "Why, Senator, I just adore it!"

The old maid bought herself a parrot to brighten her lonely hours. The parrot's name was Bobby, and he was a charming bird, with but one small fault. Whenever the mild-mannered lady had company in, Bobby would cut loose with a number of obscene expressions he'd picked up from his previous owner, a retired madam.

The lady discussed this problem with her pastor, and after witnessing a particularly purple display, the good man suggested, "This parrot needs company. Get him interested in another of his species, and he'll soon forget his sinful past.

"I, myself, have a parrot. Her name is Sarah and she is an unusually devout bird. She *prays* constantly. Let me bring her with me the next time I call. We'll keep them together a few days—I'm certain her religious background will have a marked influence on

*"Miss Cummings is out, but if you'd
care to come in anyway, I think
I know what to do."*

this fellow's character."

Thus, the next time the pastor called, he brought his parrot, and the two birds were placed in a single cage. They spent the first couple of minutes hopping about and sizing one another up, then Bobby spoke:

"I go for you, sweetie," he whistled. "How about you and me shacking up?!"

"You betcha, big boy," said Sarah. "Whatcha think I've been *praying* for?!"


We are scholars. Yes, we are. We recently traced the origin of the expression, "Hurrah for our side!" back to the crowds lining the streets when Lady Godiva made her famous ride sidesaddle through the streets of Coventry.


A big-store buyer had been on the road for nearly two months. Each week he would send his wife a telegram saying: "Can't come home yet. Still buying."

His wife knew that these buying trips usually involved more than business. She tolerated this particular jaunt for a while, but when the third month rolled by and she'd still seen nothing of her husband but the weekly telegrams, she wired him: "Better come home. I'm selling what you're buying."


The husband was disturbed by his wife's indifferent attitude toward him and the marriage counselor suggested he try being more aggressive in his love-making.

"Act more like a romantic lover and less like a

48

*"I have to rent a furnished room for a week.*
*My mother is coming to visit me."*

bored spouse," he was advised. "When you go home, make love to her as soon as you meet—even if it is right inside the front door."

At the next consultation, the advisor was pleased to hear that the husband had followed instructions. "And how did she react this time?" the consultant asked.

"Well, to tell the truth," the husband replied, "she was still sort of indifferent. But one thing I've got to admit: her bridge club went absolutely wild!"


**"W**hy don't you smile?" the teacher asked young Johnny.

"I didn't have no breakfast," Johnny replied.

"You poor dear," said the teacher. "But to return to our geography lesson, Johnny: where is the Polish border?"

"In bed with Momma—that's why I didn't have no breakfast."


**A** salesman friend of ours spent a couple of days in Miami last fall. His first night there, a good-looking blonde approached him in a bar and said, "I'm selling —you buying?"

Our friend bought and thought no more about it till, a week later, he discovered he had a "case."

He visited a doctor and had it taken care of, and two months later business again took him to Miami and again he visited the same bar. Sure enough, the same blonde was there, and once again she approached him with, "I'm selling—you buying?"

"Well, that depends," said our friend, sipping his drink thoughtfully. "What are you selling tonight—cancer?"

Some girls go out every Saturday night and sow wild oats, then go to church on Sunday and pray for a crop failure.

The aging playboy should find some satisfaction in the knowledge that though he's not as good as he once was, he's as good once as he once was.

One by one, the vice-presidents of a large corporation were called into the boss' office. Then the junior executives were individually summoned. Finally the office boy was brought in.

"I want the truth, Charles," the boss bellowed. "Have you been playing around with my secretary?"

"N-no, sir," the office boy stammered, "I-I'd never

do anything like that, sir."

"All right, all right," said the boss, "then *you* fire her."

The new American ambassador to the Far Eastern country called on the Emperor to present his credentials. During his official visit, he was disturbed by the presence of a number of comely, near-nude maidens wandering about the palace, but hoping to restrict the conversation to matters of state, he asked, "Your Highness, when was the last time you had an election here?"

"Ah," said the Emperor with a smile and a sly wink, "just befo' blekfast."

An inmate at the insane asylum was being examined for possible release. The first question the examining doctor asked was: "What are you going to do when you leave this institution?"

"I'm gonna get me a slingshot," said the patient, "and I'm gonna come back here and break every goddamned window in the place!"

After six more months of treatment, the patient was again brought before the examining doctor for possible dismissal, and the same question was put to him.

"Well, I'm going to get a job," the patient replied.

"Fine," said the doctor. "Then what?"

"I'm going to rent an apartment."

"Very good."

"... You don't see crime in our fair city
under Mayor Hale ... you don't see graft
under Mayor Hale ... you don't
see prostitutes under ..."

"Then I'm going to meet a beautiful girl."

"Excellent."

"I'm going to take the beautiful girl up to my apartment and I'm going to pull up her skirt."

"Normal, perfectly normal."

"Then I'm gonna steal her garter, make a slingshot out of it, and come back here and break every goddamned window in the place!"

We overheard a couple of modern young ladies chatting at cocktails the other afternoon. "Did you hear about Joanne getting married again?" asked the first.

"No!" exclaimed the other in surprise. "I didn't even know she was pregnant."

The couple stepped up to the desk clerk of one of the city's nicer hotels. "I'd like a room and bath for my wife and myself," said the gentleman.

"I'm terribly sorry, sir," said the clerk, "but the only room available doesn't have bathroom facilities."

"Will that be all right with you, dear?" the gentleman asked the young lady at his side.

"Sure, mister," she said.

When a French Lady Representative managed to close all the brothels in France after the war, they promptly opened up again as private clubs. Shortly afterward an elderly gentleman, unaware of the change, knocked at the door of one of the "clubs." Having been instructed to maintain the impression that

"It seems like only yesterday she was
crying for her oatmeal."

he was working for a private club, the doorman first asked: "Active member?"

"I hope so," the old man replied.

The young man addressed his prospective father-in-law: "Sir, I would like to marry your daughter."

"I'm afraid, son," the older man replied, "that you couldn't support her in the manner to which she is accustomed."

"Your daughter and I have talked it over, and she has consented to live on what I earn."

"That's fine. But remember that after a while a little one may come along, and that will mean added expense."

"Well, that's true, sir," the youth agreed, "but we've been lucky so far."

A young man was out on a first date with a rather flat-chested girl. The evening ended on the sofa in the young lady's parlor. The boy put his arm around her and made a few preliminary passes.

The girl stiffened indignantly. "Here, here!" she exclaimed.

"Where, where?" he replied.

"Darling," she whispered, "will you still love me after we are married?"

He considered this for a moment and then replied, "I think so. I've always been especially fond of married women."

The sophisticated lady was approached on the dance floor by a gentleman slightly her junior.

"I'm sorry," she said in a superior tone, "but I couldn't dance with a child."

"Oh, I'm sorry," he said. "I didn't know your condition."

We've always been partial to absent-minded professor jokes. Like the one about the guy who walked into the men's room, unbuttoned his vest, and pulled out his necktie.

Two Englishmen struck up a conversation with an American in the club car of a train headed east out of Chicago.

"I say," queried the younger Englishman, "have you ever been to London?"

The American laughed. "It was my home for two years during the war," he said. "Had some of the wildest times of my life in that old town."

The older Englishman, a little hard of hearing, asked, "What did he say, Reggie?"

"He said he's been to London, father," the younger Englishman replied.

After a little lull in the conversation, the young man asked, "You didn't, by any chance, meet a Hazel Wimbleton in London, did you?"

The American almost fell off his chair. "Hot-Pants Hazel?!" he exclaimed. "My God, I shacked up with that broad for three months just before I came back to the States."

"What did he say, Reggie?" the older Englishman wanted to know.

"He says he knows mother," the younger Englishman responded.

The prudish old maid found herself seated next to a sophisticated playboy at a formal affair. After a little, rather icy conversation, the lady attempted to dismiss

*"It would be a much better act if
she trusted him more."*

the fellow with, "It's quite obvious, sir, that we do not agree on a single, solitary thing."

The playboy smiled. "Oh, I don't think that's quite true, madam," he said. "If you were to enter a bedroom in which there were two beds, and if, madam, there were a woman in one and a man in the other, in which bed would you sleep?"

"Well," the lady huffed indignantly, "with the woman, of course."

"You see, we agree," the playboy said laughing. "So would I."

The ship's captain returned from a two-year voyage to find his wife nursing a month-old baby. "Who did this?" he demanded. "Was it my friend Mike Fitzpatrick?"

"No," his wife said softly.

"Well then, was it my friend Bob Bigelow?"

His wife shook her head.

"Bill Connery," he demanded, "could it have been my friend Bill Connery?"

"*Your* friends, *your* friends," his wife said impatiently, "all the time, *your* friends. Don't you think I have any friends of my own?"

A wise man has observed that people who live in glass houses shouldn't.

Maybe you heard about the drunk who was staggering through the park and saw a young athlete practicing

*"I guess we're through—she returned
everything I gave her."*

push-ups. "Washamatter, Mac?" inquired the lush. "Lose your girl?"

**T**hen there was the playboy who suddenly decided to live a strictly moral life. First, he cut out smoking. Then he cut out liquor. Then he cut out swearing. Then he cut out women.

Now he's cutting out paper dolls.

**T**he unusually high birth rate in a suburb near our city was recently explained to us. Every morning at 6:15 the Express comes roaring through town blowing its whistle.

It's too early to get out of bed and too late to go back to sleep.

**T**he two office workers were complaining about the short lunch hours.

"The boss takes an hour-and-a-half every day and expects us to get by on 30 minutes," said Tom.

"If I had an extra 15, I could go home for lunch," agreed Bill.

"The boss is never around at noon. Why don't we just *take* the extra 15 minutes," Tom suggested.

Bill agreed and that very day he went home for lunch. Naturally his wife wasn't expecting him and when he didn't find her in the front part of the house, Bill looked in the bedroom. When he opened the door, he discovered his wife in bed with his boss. Bill backed out of the room quietly, slipped out of the house without being noticed and hurried back to the office.

The following morning Tom asked him if he was going to take the extra 15 minutes again that day.

"Hell, no," said Bill. "I almost got caught yesterday."

Returning from the funeral of his beautiful wife, the widower was disconsolate.

"I know how deeply grieved you are," his best friend said, "but you're young and in time you will forget. You'll meet someone else with whom you will share real happiness."

"I know, I know," said the husband, "but what about *tonight*?"

**G**ood heavens, Doctor! What a terrific bill," the patient protested.

"My dear fellow," the doctor replied, "if you knew what an interesting case yours was, and how strongly I was tempted to let it proceed to a post-mortem, you wouldn't complain at a bill three times as big as this."

**A** father was shopping in a department store with his small daughter, when the little girl suddenly pulled on his coat sleeve and said, "Daddy, I gotta go."

"In a few minutes, dear," the father replied.

"I gotta go *now*," the little girl insisted in a very loud voice.

To avoid a scene, a saleslady stepped forward and said, "That's all right, sir, I'll take her."

The saleslady and the little girl hurried off hand in hand. When they returned, the father asked his daughter, "Did you thank the nice lady for being so kind?"

"Why should I thank her?" retorted the little girl, as loud as before. "She had to go, too."

**L**ittle Johnny, with a grin,
Drank up all of pappy's gin.
Mother said, when he was plastered,
"Go to bed, you little love-child."

*"Shall we join them?"*

"That man made love to me, Judge," said the plaintiff in the breach-of-promise suit. "He promised to marry me, and then he married another woman. He broke my heart and I want $10,000."

She got it.

The next case was a damage suit brought by a woman who had been run over by an automobile and had three ribs broken. She was awarded $300.

Moral: Don't break their hearts, kick 'em in the ribs.

The old bull's active days were over, but the kindly farmer permitted him to stay on in the pasture with the cows. Of course, the farmer also turned a young bull loose in the field and the newcomer went to work immediately. Seeing this, the old bull began snorting and pawing the ground with his hoof.

"You're wasting your time," said the farmer. "You're too old for that sort of thing now."

"I know," said the bull, "but I can show him I'm not a cow, can't I?"

Mrs. Applebottom grew angry with the French maid and after a series of stinging remarks regarding the young girl's abilities as a cook and housekeeper, she dismissed her. But the girl's Gallic ancestry wouldn't allow such abuse to go unanswered: "Your husband considers me a better cook and housekeeper than you, Madam. He has told me so himself."

Mrs. Applebottom looked at the girl scornfully and

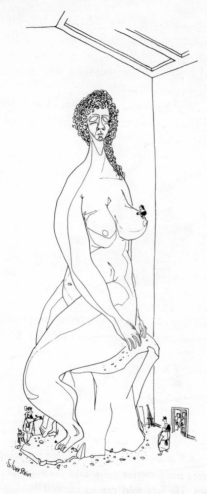

*"Irwin . . . !"*

made no comment.

"And furthermore," said the angry girl, "I am better than you in the bed!"

"And I suppose my husband told you that, too," snapped Mrs. Applebottom.

"No, Madam," said the maid, "the chauffeur told me *that*!"

**H**eard tell about the widow who wears black garters in remembrance of those who have passed beyond.

**"H**ow many beers does it take to make you dizzy?" he asked.

"Four or five," she retorted, "and don't call me Dizzy!"

**P**ete was the playboy of the office. He kept the typewriter set bug-eyed with juicy tales of his conquests. One afternoon a bachelor in the office cornered him and asked, "Pete, how the hell do you do it? You're a married man, but you make Casanova look like a two-bit amateur. Come on, buddy, what's your secret?"

Pete was in a conversational mood. "I wouldn't do this for everybody, Eddie," he said, "but you're a friend, so I'll tell you my secret. Like all great plans, it's really very simple. It's all in the *approach*!

"Tonight, take the 5:21 out of Penn Station and get off at Great Neck. You'll find dozens of dolls there waiting for their husbands. Now there are always *some* husbands who have to work late. So all you have to do is be charming and let nature take its course."

The system was indeed simple, but it also seemed foolproof. Eddie boarded the 5:21 that night with Pete's instructions fixed firmly in his mind. But he dozed en route and didn't waken till two stops after Great Neck. He got off the train in a hurry and was about to catch a cab back to his destination when he noticed an unescorted female standing on the platform looking very, very available.

He sauntered over casually, lit her cigarette, and asked whether she'd like to have a nice quiet drink with him.

"I'd love to," she said, "but let's go to my place. It's near here and it's very, very quiet."

Everything went as planned. They had a small dinner at her place, some drinks, then they retired to the pleasures of the bedroom. They'd been enjoying themselves only a few minutes, however, when the door swung open and the lady's husband entered.

"Goddamnit, Betty," he cried, "what the hell goes on here?! So this is what you do when my back is turned! And as for you, you muttonhead—I thought I told you to get off at Great Neck!!"

For her first week's salary, the gorgeous new secretary was given an exquisite nightgown of imported lace. The next week her salary was raised.

Mary had a little sheep,
And with the sheep she went to sleep.
The sheep turned out to be a ram—
Mary had a little lamb.

Last summer a friend of ours vacationed at a popular resort where he met a young and charming girl. She prided herself on being a good sport and demonstrated this by enjoying just about everything with our friend —dining, dancing, swimming, tennis, horseback riding, motoring—just about everything, in short, except that special enjoyment he was really interested in.

"Oh, come on," he entreated, "you're always saying what a good sport you are. Why draw the line at this?" Appealing to her sense of good sportsmanship finally turned the trick, and the last evening of their vacation was the most enjoyable of all.

Back on the job, our friend had almost forgotten the incident when, just a week ago, the phone rang.

"Do you know who this is?" a sweet, feminine voice asked.

He didn't, of course.

"The girl from the lake this summer," she said.

*"The honeymoon turned out so nice we
decided to get married."*

"The good sport."

She said she had something important to tell him and wanted to meet him for a drink after work. Remembering the pleasant interlude at the end of their vacation, he made a date for that very evening.

Over manhattans, the girl confided that she was in a family way and asked him what he was going to do about it.

Our friend was understandably unnerved.

"I—I don't know what I *can* do," he said, gulping down his drink. "This summer was just for laughs. I'm engaged to be married to another girl. The question is, what are *you* going to do about it?"

"Well," she said, almost in tears, "I suppose I could kill myself!"

"Gee!" He breathed a sigh of relief. "You *are* a good sport!"


The evening had been going very well, but now, at the critical moment, the girl wouldn't let the playboy into her apartment. Her excuse was thin: "My roommate's home."

Bitter, her date said, "In other words, I'm supposed to ignore this door mat that says *Welcome*?"

"Of course, silly," she laughed. "There certainly isn't room enough for us on that!"


The young bride's mother had some old-fashioned ideas of marriage and passed them on to her daughter. "Never let your husband see you in the nude," she ad-

"Jeannie—what's the past tense of 'virgin'?"

vised. "You should always wear something."

"Yes, Mother," replied the obedient girl.

Two weeks after the wedding, the girl and her brand-new husband were preparing to retire when the fellow asked, "Dear, has there ever been any insanity in your family?"

"Not that I know of," she answered. "Why?"

"Well," said her husband, "we've been married two weeks now and every night you've worn that silly hat to bed."

One of the executive secretaries had just returned from her honeymoon and was discussing it with the girls at the office.

"How did your husband register at the hotel?" one little co-worker wanted to know.

"Fine," the secretary said, beaming. "Just fine!"

"I believe you have the wrong number," said the old gentleman into the phone. "You'll have to call the weather bureau for that information."

"Who was that?" his young wife asked.

"Some guy wanting to know if the coast was clear."

**T**he romantic young man sat on the park bench with a first date. He was certain his charming words and manner would win her as they had so many others.

"Some moon out tonight," he cooed.

"There certainly is," she agreed.

"Some really bright stars in the sky."

She nodded.

"Some dew on the grass."

"*Some* do," she said indignantly, "but *I'm* not that sort!"

**T**he very proper spinster didn't go out very often, but she'd had some important shopping to do that morning and so decided to have her lunch in what appeared to be a nice and quite respectable restaurant. With the noontime crowd, many customers shared their tables with strangers: the spinster selected a seat next to an attractive, young office girl. The girl finished her sandwich and coffee, then settled back and lit up a cigarette. The older woman controlled herself for a few moments and then snapped, "I'd rather commit adultery than smoke in public."

"So would I," said the girl, "but I only have half-an-hour for lunch."

The young man took his girl to an open-air theater on their first date. After the first act he found it necessary to excuse himself. He asked the usher where the men's room was located and was told, "turn left by that big oak tree, go straight ahead about 20 yards, then right another five."

In a few minutes he returned to his seat.

"Has the second act started yet?" he asked his date.

"You ought to know," she said coolly. "You were in it!"

The two television actors feigned friendship, but secretly hated each other's guts, and took great pleasure in giving one another the needle on any and all occasions. This particular evening they met, quite by accident, at a popular bar just off Broadway. The conversation started innocently enough, then one, with sudden inspiration, ran his hand over the other's bald head, and exclaimed: "By God, Fred, that feels just like my wife's derriere!"

The other ran his own hand over his head, and non-

chalantly retorted: "Well, I'll be damned, Jim, so it does, so it does!"

The circus was finishing its final performance in the country town when one of its zebras had a stroke. The local veterinarian prescribed a few weeks rest for the beast, so the circus owner made arrangements to board it at a nearby farm.

The zebra took to the new life immediately and spent the first day meeting all the animals of the barnyard.

He came across a chicken and said, "I'm a zebra, who are you?"

"I'm a chicken," said the chicken.

"What do you do?" asked the zebra.

"I scratch around and lay eggs," said the chicken.

Moving on, the zebra found a cow. He introduced himself saying, "I'm a zebra. Who are you?"

"I'm a cow," said the cow.

"What do you do?" asked the zebra.

"I graze in the field and give milk," said the cow.

The zebra met a bull next. "I'm a zebra," he said. "Who are you?"

"I'm a bull," said the bull.

"And what do you do?" asked the zebra.

"What do I do!" snorted the bull, pawing at the turf with a forefoot. "Why you silly-looking ass—take off your pajamas and I'll show you!"

"I've learned one thing about women," said the ex-

*"Here's a quarter to stick around. I may need your help later."*

perienced one to his drinking companions. "You just can't trust a girl with brown eyes."

"It occurs to me," said one of his inebriated friends, "that I've been married nearly three years and I don't know what color eyes my wife has."

The second man finished his drink, climbed from his stool and hurried home to investigate this disturbing possibility. His wife was in bed asleep. He crept up to her and carefully lifted an eyelid.

"By God! *Brown!*" he exclaimed.

"How the hell did you know I was here," said Brown, crawling out from under the bed.

A sweet young schoolteacher who had always been virtuous was invited to go for a ride in the country with the gym instructor, whom she admired. Under a tree on the bank of a quiet lake, she struggled with her conscience and with the gym instructor and finally gave in to the latter. Sobbing uncontrollably, she asked her seducer, "How can I ever face my students again, knowing I have sinned twice?"

"Twice?" asked the young man confused.

"Why, yes," said the sweet teacher, wiping a tear from her eye, "you're going to do it again, aren't you?"

The preacher's sermon was on the Ten Commandments. When he reached the fourth, "Thou Shalt Not Steal," he noticed one of his parishioners, a little man sitting in the front row, became very agitated. When the preacher reached the seventh, "Thou Shalt Not

Commit Adultery," the man suddenly smiled and relaxed.

After the service, the preacher approached the man and asked him the reason for his peculiar behavior.

The man replied with an embarrassed smile, "When you talked about the Fourth Commandment, 'Thou Shalt Not Steal,' I suddenly discovered my umbrella was missing. But when you said 'Thou Shalt Not Commit Adultery,' I remembered where I'd left it."

**A**n old-fashioned gentleman took a modern miss for a ride in his car and after finding a suitable spot to park, kissed her several times lightly on the cheek and then announced, "This is called *spooning*."

"OK," she said, "but I think I'd rather *shovel*."

**A** business friend was trying to convince us the other day that sex is so popular because it's centrally located.

**U**pon applying for admission to one of the most exclusive country clubs in New England, the rather reserved, unimpressive-looking young man was notified that he must play a round of golf with the club officers as a prerequisite to his acceptance.

On the appointed afternoon, he met them on the first tee equipped with a hockey stick, a croquet mallet and a billiard cue. The officers looked him over incredulously, but nevertheless proceeded to tee off. To their dismay, the young man coolly drove 310 yards with the hockey stick, gracefully arched his second shot to the green with the croquet mallet and sank a 20-foot putt with the billiard cue.

After soundly drubbing the baffled officers with a sub-par 68, the applicant retired with them to the club bar. There he ordered a Scotch and soda, and when it arrived, he mixed the drink himself by tossing the contents of the shot glass over his shoulder into the waiting soda behind him on the bar. This further display of the young man's incredible physical coordination was too much for the officers of the club.

"You're miraculous," they exclaimed. "What's the story behind these fantastic talents of yours?"

"All my life," the man explained, "physical activity of any sort has been child's play for me. To overcome the boredom that has resulted from my monotonous mastery of everything, I try to do almost everything in the most difficult way possible. Thus, I play tennis with a Ping-Pong paddle, Ping-Pong with a tennis racket, and so on."

"Wait a minute," interrupted one of the club officers. "If it's true, as you say, that you do everything

*"P, L, X, S, F, Y."*

physical in the most difficult manner possible, I have one question . . ."

"I know," said the talented young man, smiling. "Everyone asks me the same thing and I don't mind telling you. Standing up . . . in a hammock."

"Doctor," said the man on the phone, "my son has scarlet fever."

"Yes, I know," replied the doctor. "I came by your house and treated him yesterday. Just keep him away from the others in the house and . . ."

"But you don't understand," said the distraught parent. "He's kissed the maid!"

"Well, that's unfortunate. Now we'll probably have to quarantine her . . ."

"And, doctor, I'm afraid I've kissed the girl myself."

"This is getting complicated. That means you may have contracted the disease."

"Yes, and I've kissed my wife since then."

"Damn it," exclaimed the doctor, "now I'll catch it, too!"

A director was interviewing a pretty young actress who had just arrived in Hollywood from the East. After the usual questions, he looked her up and down and asked, "Are you a virgin?"

She nodded, then realizing a job might hinge on her answer, she added, "But I'm not a fanatic about it!"

An elderly gentleman visited his doctor with the com-

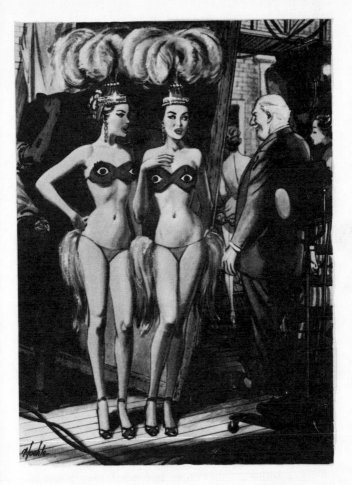

*"Watch him—he likes to sneak up behind a
girl and play 'Guess Who?'!"*

plaint that he believed he was becoming impotent.

"When did you first become aware of this problem?" the doctor asked.

The old gentleman replied, "Yesterday afternoon, twice last night and again this morning."

**A** man was complaining to a friend about an uncle who was staying with him: "I didn't mind when he wore my suits, I didn't object when he smoked my best cigars, drank my bourbon and borrowed my car every night. But when he sat down at the dinner table and laughed at me with my own teeth—that was too much!"

**T**he husband finally wised up to the fact that his wife was something less than faithful. He put a private investigator on her tail, and within a week had the name and address of the "other man."

"No sonofabitch is going to break up my home," the husband snarled indignantly to himself. "My loving wife would be true to me today, if this sneaky guy hadn't come on the scene!"

Still, the husband prided himself on his sophistication, and determined to handle the situation in a businesslike way. He called in his secretary and dictated this letter:

Sir: It has been called to my attention that for some time now you have been carrying on an affair with my wife. So that we can settle this matter intelligently, please see me in my office at three P.M. sharp on Friday.

The "other man," amused by the husband's formal manner, called in his own secretary and dictated this reply:

Dear Sir: Received your circular letter this morning. You are advised that I will attend the scheduled conference on time.

**T**hree Frenchmen were discussing the meaning of the word *savoir-faire*. The first explained, "If you come home and discover your wife in another man's arms and you say, 'Excuse me,' that's *savoir-faire*."

"No, no," said another who was slightly older and more experienced, "that's not quite right. If you come home and find your wife in another man's arms and you say, 'Excuse me, proceed,' that's *savoir-faire!*"

The third Frenchman was still older and wiser, and he said, with a smile, "I'm afraid neither of you really understands the full meaning of the word. If you come home and discover your wife in the arms of another man and you say, 'Excuse me, proceed,' and he proceeds, then *he* has *savoir-faire*."

The judge looked down at the sweet young thing. "You claim that the defendant stole your money from your stocking?" he asked.

"That's right, Your Honor," she answered.

"Well, why didn't you resist?" the judge asked.

The girl blushed and lowered her eyes. "I didn't know he was after my money, Your Honor," she said.

The two old maids lived their lonely lives together until, rather unexpectedly, a stranger arrived on the scene and whisked one of them away in matrimony. After the honeymoon, the new bride visited her unmarried friend and painted an ecstatic picture of married life.

"Our honeymoon," she said, "was like a cruise down the Mediterranean, a sail into a glorious sunset. It was *wonderful!*"

The second old maid was very much impressed and

*"I told you if we were late we'd
miss all the fun."*

determined to get a man for herself. She showed her bankbook around town and eventually nailed a local gigolo. They were married at once and began their honeymoon.

They climbed into their wedding bed and in a short time the husband was flushed with excitement. The bride, however, was cool as a cucumber and decidedly unaffected by the proceedings.

"I simply don't understand it," she said rather indignantly. "My friend told me that marriage was like a cruise down the Mediterranean—like a sail into a glorious sunset."

"Oh, she did, eh?" said the guy, now trembling with uncontrollable excitement. "Well *bon voyage* baby— I'm sailing without you!"


The French executive was traveling home by rail from a Paris business conference. As he pulled aside the curtains of his berth, he discovered two beautiful girls there. A glance at their tickets told him that the girls were in the wrong car. Distressed, the beauties flashed their most melting smiles and asked if they might stay where they were.

"My dear ladies," explained the executive, "I am a married man, a pillar of my community, and scandal has never touched me. *One* of you," he concluded, "will have to leave."


The Southern boy was trying to make time up North. "Honey chile," he purred to a luscious Yankee, "would

*"It was owned by an elderly couple."*

it be all right if Ah kissed yo' all?"

Snapped she: "Aren't my lips enough?"

---

As Sam the fruit man reminded us the other day, the apple of the average playboy's eye is usually the prettiest peach with the biggest pear.

---

Crazy Charlie, the used-car dealer, was out to break all sales records with his "like new" models. A large sign in his window announced: A BLONDE FREE WITH EACH CAR.

A delighted young wolf plunked down his cash and, hot with anticipation, drove his newly won blonde out into the country. He parked, gave her a couple of preliminary kisses and whispered a suggestion in her ear.

She shook her head, smiled and said, "You got that when you bought this car."

"Here's how," said the playboy, raising his glass.

"Say *when*," said his date. "I know *how*!"

A young man met his ex-wife at a party and after a few drinks, he suggested that they have another try at marriage.

"Over my dead body," she sneered.

He downed his drink, and replied, "I see you haven't changed a bit."

The connoisseur sat down at the bar and ordered a martini. "Very dry," he insisted. "Twenty parts gin to one part vermouth."

"All right, sir," said the bartender. "Shall I twist a bit of lemon peel over it?"

"My good man, when I want lemonade, I'll ask for it."

"Will you have a drink?" the young man asked.

"I don't drink," his date replied.

"May I offer you a cigarette?"

"I don't smoke," she said.

"Would you be interested in going up to my apartment, putting a little mood music on the phonograph and . . ." She answered by slapping his face.

"I don't suppose you eat hay either," he said, nursing his jaw.

"Well, hardly," she said icily.

"Just as I thought," he sighed. "Not fit company for man or beast."

**A** table of improper measures we came upon the other day informs us that it takes two pints to make one cavort.

**G**irls get minks the same way minks get minks.

**D**uring a recent expedition into the wildest part of darkest Africa, a group of explorers came upon a village of primitive savages. In an attempt to make friends, the leader of the explorers tried to tell the natives what it was like in the civilized, outside world.

"Out there," he said, "we love our fellow man."

To this, the natives gave a ringing cry of "*Huzzanga!*"

Encouraged by this, the explorer continued: "We treat others as we would want them to treat us!"

"*Huzzanga!*" exclaimed the natives, with much enthusiasm.

"We are peaceful!" said the explorer.

"*Huzzanga!*" cried the natives.

With a tear running down his cheek, the explorer ended his fine speech: "We come to you as friends, as brothers. So trust us. Open your arms to us, your

"Sure, I saw them, but I thought it was
something by Rodin."

houses, your hearts. What do you say?"

The air shook with one long, mighty *"Huzzanga!"*

Greatly pleased by the reception, the leader of the explorers then began talking with the natives' chief.

"I see that you have cattle here," he said. "They are a species with which I'm unfamiliar. May I inspect them?"

"Certainly, come this way," said the chief. "But be careful not to step in the huzzanga."

An elderly playboy we know has cataloged the three stages of a man's life: Tri-Weekly, Try Weekly, Try Weakly.

An old roué of our acquaintance recently pointed out that about the only thing you can look down on and approve of at the same time is a plunging neckline.

Alfred had been married to lovely Arlene for less than a year and already he was beginning to suspect she was untrue to him.

Forced to leave town for the weekend on a business trip, Alfred explained the problem to his close friend, Wendell, and asked him to keep an eye on his wife while he was away.

Upon his return, Alfred demanded a complete account of Arlene's activities.

"Well," Wendell said, "the night you left a good-looking guy came over to the house. Arlene got all dressed up and they went out to a night club. I fol-

*"Most men your age would be satisfied with a little peace of __mind__!"*

lowed them and saw them drinking together and dancing very closely. Finally around three in the morning, they got into a cab and I could see them hugging and kissing in the back seat. I followed them back to your house and watched through the living-room window while they mixed more drinks and hugged and kissed each other some more. Then they went into the bedroom and they switched out the lights, so I couldn't see anymore."

"That's the trouble," exclaimed Alfred. "Always that element of doubt!"

Then there were the two honeymooners who wanted to fly United, but the stewardess wouldn't let them.

While dancing with a dapper Englishman, the American girl's brooch became unfastened and slid down the back of her gown.

She told her escort about it and asked him to retrieve the lost article. Somewhat embarrassed, but determined to please, he reached cautiously down the back of her gown. After a moment, he said, "Awfully sorry, but I can't seem to locate it."

"Try farther down," she advised. He did, beginning to blush. Still no brooch. "Down still farther," she ordered.

Looking around and discovering that he was being watched by every couple on the dance floor, the Englishman blushed even deeper and whispered, "I feel a perfect ass."

"*Never mind that!*" she snapped. "Just get the brooch!"

The sexy redhead was telling her roommate about an unusual experience she'd had on a date the night before.

"George asked me to pose for him," she said, "in the nude."

"And of course you told him you're not a model," countered the roommate.

"Of course," said the redhead, "but he said that didn't matter, because he's not an artist."

A wealthy gentleman was badly bitten by bugs while riding on a certain railway line. Arriving at his destination, he wrote the company an indignant letter and received a prompt reply. It was, said the letter, the first complaint the company had ever had of this nature. Inquiry had failed to reveal any explanation for this unprecedented occurrence. Nevertheless, a number of new precautions were being taken to make absolutely certain such an unfortunate incident never happened again. The letter was signed by a high official of the railway.

The gentleman was well-satisfied with this reply and was returning it to its envelope when a slip of paper fell out onto the floor. The hastily scribbled note on it read: "Send this guy the bug letter."


The best-dressed woman at a recent society ball was the lovely Miss Agnes S. Stevens, whose gown was cut so low in back it revealed her initials.


His Lordship awoke with an all-too-infrequent feeling of virility and joyfully announced his condition to his valet. Impressed, the servant asked, "Shall I notify M'lady?"

"No, just hand me my baggy tweeds," replied His Lordship. "I shall smuggle this one into town."


I met a woman who was willin'— Now I'm usin' penicillin.


"I'm going to have a little one,"
Said the girl, so gay and frisky.
And the boyfriend up and fainted.
(Then she told him she meant whiskey).


The big-city sporting houses were hard hit by the hous-

"Well, she's about your _height_,
but—uh—smaller."

ing shortage. One of them became so crowded on busy nights that it was obliged to entertain some of its customers on the roof. On one such evening, a client and his charming hostess became so excited they fell off the top of the building. Still locked in love's embrace, they landed on the street with a thud, barely missing a passing drunk.

The drunk staggered up to the sporting-house door and knocked loud and long.

"Beat it," said the madam through a slot in the door. "We don't allow no drunks in here."

"I don't wanna come in," said the drunk. "Jush wanted to tell ya your sign fell down."


**A** young virgin, suffering from acute nervousness due to repressed desires, paid a visit to a highly recommended psychiatrist. The doctor took one look at the voluptuous maiden and lost all his professional objectivity. "Take off your clothes," he ordered, scarcely able to disguise the lust in his voice. "Now lie down on this couch. Now close your eyes and very slowly spell the word, 'bedroom.'"

She began: "B . . . E . . . D . . . R . . . *Oh!* . . . *Ohhhh* . . . *Mmmmmmmmmmmmmmmm.*"

She was cured.


**A** stranger in town found his way to the most luxurious bordello. He entered, selected a gorgeous redhead and was escorted to a resplendent bedchamber of Hollywood proportions. Half-an-hour later, a satisfied

*"Well, we'll give it a try, but I don't think many men carry two dollars in change."*

smile on his face, he sought out the madam and took his wallet from his pocket. But the madam would not accept payment. She opened the drawer of a solid-gold cash register, counted out $100 and handed the money to him. Stunned and speechless, he staggered out.

A week later, he returned, chose a succulent blonde, and was presented with $200 by the madam. Still puzzled, he took the money and left, feeling himself a very lucky fellow indeed.

The next night, he decided to pay another visit. After enjoying the services of a beautiful brunette, he walked up to the madam, held out his hand and waited for the money. He was unpleasantly surprised when she said, "Twenty-five dollars, please."

"Now, look here," he rejoined. "The first time I came here, *you* gave *me* $100. The second time, you gave me $200. How come I didn't get paid tonight?"

"Tonight," replied the madam, "you were *not* on television!"

Some girls go to such lengths to get a mink coat that when they finally get one, they have trouble buttoning it.

Two farmers were discussing their sons' progress in the big-city university. Ezra said, "I don't rightly understand them *degrees* the boys are workin' fer. Do you, Cy?"

"Reckon so," replied Cy, modestly. "First one they

get is called a B. S. And you know what that means."

Being a man of the world, Ezra knew.

Cy went on: "Well, sir, they work a little harder and they get this here M.S. That means More of the Same."

Ezra nodded.

"Then comes the hard part. They study night and day, put in years of readin', write all kinds of papers, and then, if they're lucky, they get the highest one of 'em all. The Ph.D."

"And what does that stand fer?" asked Ezra.

"Piled Higher and Deeper."

We just overheard a couple of our pretty stenographers discussing one of the more dashing members of our staff. "He dresses so well," said one.

"And so quickly," replied the other.

Three French boys, ages 8, 10 and 12, were walking together down a Paris street and, passing an open window where a young bride and groom were consummating their marriage, stopped to watch. "Observe!" said the 8-year-old. "That lady and gentleman are fighting!"

"You are mistaken," said the 10-year-old, both older and more sophisticated than his comrade. "They are making love."

"*Oui*," said the 12-year-old. "And badly."


**T**he fellows were kidding the one married man among them. "You've been married five years now, George," one of them said. "How come you have no children? Is your wife" (and here he tried a very bad pun) "*unbearable*?"

"Or," interjected another, "is she inconceivable?"

"Maybe she's, uh, impregnable," joked a third.

The married man shook his head. "No, boys, you're all wrong. She's insurmountable and inscrutable."


**"A** man is responsible for the good name of his family," said the lecturer grandly. "Is there a man among us who would let his wife be slandered and not rise to her defense?"

One meek little fellow in the back of the room stood up.

"What's this?" exclaimed the speaker. "You sir— would you permit your wife to be slandered and not protest?!"

"Oh," apologized the little fellow, resuming his seat, "I thought you said 'slaughtered.'"

*"Sarah certainly is a friend of the
downtrodden."*

A few friends had gathered in Bob's basement rec room for an evening of drinks and dancing. With the party in full swing, one of the girls excused herself to go to the john. This room, it seems, had been newly painted in a charming pastel blue; it was supposed to be a fast-drying enamel, but it hadn't dried fast enough, and the young lady found herself stuck. Her shrieks brought Joe's girlfriend, who, unable to do anything about the situation herself, summoned Joe. After several minutes of uncontrolled laughter, Joe managed to produce a screw-driver and detach the thing, permitting the girl to stand up. But they still couldn't get it off, so they called a doctor.

"Did you ever see anything like this before, doctor?" the girl asked in embarrassment when the M.D. arrived.

"Well, yes," the doctor replied truthfully, "but I believe this is the first time I've ever seen one framed."

A middle-aged woman stood watching a little boy on the curb smoking a cigarette and drinking from a bottle of Scotch. Finally, unable to bear it any longer, she stalked up to the lad and demanded, "Why aren't you in school at this time of day?"

"Hell, lady," said the boy, gulping again from the bottle, "I'm only four years old."

Everyone was surprised when fastidious, virginal Percy lispingly announced his intention to wed. "What, *you*, Percy?" was the amazed reaction. Some skeptics made bets that he wouldn't go through with it, but Percy

"Er—Just how far does this marriage-counseling service of yours go, Dr. Beidecker?"

fooled them. He even went on a honeymoon. Upon his return, one of the losers bitingly asked, "Well, is your wife pregnant?"

"I certainly hope so," said Percy with great sincerity. "I wouldn't want to go through *that* again!"

A friend has described a pink elephant as a beast of bourbon.

Jim Morgan had just returned from a month-long trip to New York and he met a good friend just outside his office.

"Jim," said the friend, "what's wrong? Your eyes are so red and bloodshot!"

"It happened on the trip," said Jim. "My very first evening in New York, I met this very attractive young woman in a cocktail lounge. We had a few drinks, then dinner and a show. One thing led to another and she spent the night with me at my hotel.

"When I awoke the next morning, she was sitting

on the edge of the bed crying. I asked her what was troubling her and she told me she was married and that she was very ashamed of herself.

"Well, that got me to thinking about my wife and kids back here, so we both sat there on the edge of the bed and cried for about a half hour."

"But, Jim," said the puzzled friend, "that was almost four weeks ago. What does that have to do with your eyes being bloodshot today?"

"Well, look," Jim exclaimed, "you can't sit and cry your eyes out every morning for four weeks without making them a little red!"

Our Research Department informs us that the bathroom is no longer the room where the most household accidents occur. It's the bedroom.

The four men at the card table were being bothered by an irritating kibitzer. When the troublesome talker stepped into the next room to mix a drink, one of the players suggested, "This next hand let's make up a game nobody ever heard of—he won't know what the hell we're playing and maybe that will shut him up."

When the kibitzer returned, the dealer tore the top two cards in half and gave them to the man on his right; he tore the corners off the next three cards and placed them before the next player, face up; he tore the next five cards in quarters, gave 15 pieces to the third man, four to himself and put the last piece in the center of the table.

Looking intently at four small pieces of card in his hand, the dealer said, "I have a mingle, so I think I'll bet a dollar."

The second man stared at the pasteboards scattered before him. "I have a snazzle," he announced, "so I'll raise you a dollar."

The third man folded without betting and the fourth, after due deliberation, said, "I've a farfle, so I'll just raise you two dollars."

The kibitzer shook his head slowly from side to side. "You're crazy," he said, "you're never going to beat a mingle and a snazzle with a lousy farfle."


**A** playboy is a cagy guy
Who has a lot of fun.
He samples every pretty wench
And never Mrs. one.


**W**e overheard two young ladies discussing their marriage plans on a northbound subway last week. "I un-

"*Just what kind of research is Professor Ditzelheiner doing?*"

derstand your boyfriend graduates from law school this June. I suppose you'll be getting married then."

"Oh, no, not right away," replied the other. "I want him to practice for at least a year first."

The little old lady rushed into the taxidermist and unwrapped a package containing two recently deceased monkeys. Her instructions to the proprietor were delivered in a welter of tears.

"Favorite pets . . . (blubber, sob) . . . caught cold . . . (moan) . . . don't see how I'll live without them . . . (weep, sob) . . . want to have them stuffed . . . (blubber, blubber)!"

"Of course, Madam," said the proprietor in an understanding voice, "and would you care to have them mounted?"

"Oh, no," she sobbed, "just shaking hands. They were just close friends."

It was painfully evident to the indignant father that all was not well with his attractive daughter. To his pointed questions, she tearfully admitted that motherhood was approaching and that the wealthy bachelor from the next block was responsible.

With fire in his eyes, the father charged down the street and rang the bachelor's bell. The young man answered the door and readily admitted his guilt.

"Just what do you intend doing about it?" demanded the parent.

The bachelor thought for a moment. "Well," he

said, "if it's a girl, I'll give your daughter $5000. And if it's a boy, I'll give her $10,000."

"See here," said the father, "if it's a miscarriage, will you give my daughter another chance?"

"I'm awfully sorry, Miss," said the store clerk, "but this five-dollar bill is counterfeit."

"Damn it," she exclaimed, "I've been seduced!"

The kindly old gentleman was visiting the home of his daughter. He entered the room of his two grandsons and found them busy studying at their desks. The first boy was reading a book on aviation.

"What do you want to be when you grow up?" asked the grandfather.

"A pilot, sir," said the boy.

"And what do you want to be when *you* grow up?" the old gentleman asked the second lad.

The boy looked up from the latest issue of PLAYBOY. "Nothing, sir," he said wistfully, "just growed up."

**O**ur grandmothers believed there was a destiny that shaped their ends, but modern girls put their faith in girdles.

**O**verheard in a fashionable sports-car salon: "This model has a top speed of 155 miles per hour, and she'll stop on a dime."

"What happens then?"

"A small putty knife emerges and scrapes you gently off the windshield."

**A**n old favorite which might bear one more telling is the one about the lady who visited a furniture store and asked to see a "sexual couch."

The salesman, masking his amusement, politely asked, "Don't you perhaps mean a sectional couch, madam?"

"No, no," she replied emphatically. "I'm sure my interior decorator told me I should have a sexual couch for an occasional piece in the living room."

**A**n elderly French playboy entered the door of his favorite sporting house and asked the madam if he might have an audience with Renée.

"Alas, Monsieur," replied the madam, "Renée is visiting her dear mother in Provence. Would you care to see Musette?"

The old gentleman smiled. "No, thank you, *chère Madame*, I will return another day. When do you expect Renée to be back?"

"Saturday next," said the madam. "Your devotion is to be admired. But can you not find diversion in the company of Clothilde? Or Gaby? Or the lively Yvette?"

To each suggestion, the old man shook his head. Curious, the madam asked, "Renée is, of course, charming, but what does she possess that the other girls do not?"

"Patience, *chère Madame*," he replied, "patience."


A much-traveled playboy we know says that in various stages of her life, a woman resembles the continents of the world: From 13 to 18, for example, she's like Africa—virgin territory, unexplored. From 18 to 30, she's like Asia—hot and exotic. From 30 to 45, she's like America—fully explored and free with her resources. From 45 to 55, she's like Europe—exhausted, but not without points of interest. After 55, concludes the playboy, she's like Australia—everybody knows it's down there, but nobody cares much.


Adjusting to marriage sometimes poses problems. We met a good friend of ours recently, the morning after his wedding, brooding over a drink in a local bar.

"What's the trouble?" we asked. "I should think you'd be the happiest man in the world today."

He shook his head sadly.

"What creatures of habit we are," he said. "This morning when I arose, half asleep, without thinking, I

*"Gee, that's funny—all he gave me was a <u>written</u> exam."*

pulled a five-dollar bill from my wallet and left it on the pillow."

We tried to console him—told him his wife wouldn't think anything of it.

"You don't understand," he said. "Half asleep, without thinking, she gave me three dollars change."

A certain small New England town has had exactly the same population figure for the last half-century. This amazing condition is attributed to the fact that every time a baby is born, a man leaves town.

A sharp rap on the door startled the two lovers.

"Quick, it's my husband," exclaimed the frightened woman. "Jump out the window!"

"But we're on the 13th floor," the Casanova gasped.

"Jump," cried the woman. "This is no time to be superstitious."

A drunk and his inebriated friend were sitting at a bar.

"Do you know what time it is?" asked the drunk.

"Sure," said the friend.

"Thanks," said the drunk.

Same two guys, same bar.

"Say," said the drunk, noticing a young lady seated at the other end of the bar, "isn't that Hortense?"

"I don't know," shrugged the friend, "she looks relaxed to me."

"It's my husband, but relax—he's sneaking
into your apartment across the hall."

The little girl walked into the drugstore and asked the clerk, "Do you fit men for trusses here?" Bewildered but obliging, he replied, "Why, yes, we do."

"Well, wash your hands," said the little girl. "I want a chocolate soda."

Our Research Department tells us that in the days of Queen Elizabeth I, some ladies-in-waiting liked to curl up with a good book, while others were satisfied with one of the pages.

One guy we know is so suspicious that when his wife gave birth to twins, he flew into a rage because only one of them looked like him.

And then there was the retired brassiere manufacturer who still liked to keep his hand in the business.

Of course, you've heard the definition of an emasculated dinosaur: A colossal fossil with a docile tassel.

"Blessed are the pure," a waggish friend of ours misquotes, "for they shall inhibit the earth."

The young bachelor showed up at the office with a black eye. "What the hell happened to you?" inquired his associates.

"Well," he said, "I was getting dressed this morning when a button came off my fly. I'm all thumbs when it comes to sewing, so I ran to the married woman in the next apartment and asked her if she'd sew the button on for me."

"Oho," interrupted his friends, "she thought you were getting fresh and pasted you, is that it?"

"No, no. She was very nice about it. Got out her sewing basket and went to work. Sat down in front of me and sewed on the button while I was standing there. She'd finished it up and was just biting off the thread when her husband walked in."

Before he went off to the wars, King Arthur locked his lovely wife, Guinevere, into her chastity belt. Then he summoned his loyal friend and subject, Sir Lancelot.

"Lancelot, noble knight," said Arthur, "within this sturdy belt is imprisoned the virtue of my wife. The key to this chaste treasure I will entrust to only one man in the world. To you."

Humbled before this great honor, Lancelot knelt, received his king's blessing, and took charge of the key. Arthur mounted his steed and rode off. Not half-a-mile from his castle, he heard hoofbeats behind him and turned to see Sir Lancelot riding hard to catch up with him. "What is amiss, my friend?" asked the king.

"My lord," gasped Lancelot, "you have given me the wrong key!"

A traveling salesman we know writes passionate love letters to a little farm girl in his territory. Her name is Sarah, but he always starts off his letters with: "Dear Hollyhock . . ."

We never understood this term of endearment till the other day when we came across this entry in the Farmer's Almanac: *"Hollyhock—Does well in fence corners and behind barns; not so well in beds."*

"In my last four shows," complained the Broadway actor, "I've played nothing but heels, and cads and egotistical swine."

"Yes, it's a shame," agreed his colleague. "This type-casting is ruining the American stage."

Two small mice were crouched under a table in the chorus girls' dressing room of a big Broadway show.

"Wow," exclaimed the first mouse, "have you ever seen so many gorgeous legs in your life?"

"Means nothing to me," said the second. "I'm a titmouse."

He did not drink, or smoke, or swear,
His morals were not bad;
Nor did he live a century—
He only *felt* he had.

The Olympic swimming champ got married to a beautiful girl and, on their honeymoon, treated her to an exhibition of his swimming prowess. He leaped into the hotel pool, cleaved the water with expert strokes and came up on the opposite side in a matter of seconds. His proud smile faded slightly when his lovely wife dived in and repeated his feat in half the time.

But, masking his bruised ego, he took her in his arms and exclaimed, "Darling, you're wonderful! Why didn't you tell me you were a swimming champion, too?"

"I'm not," she replied. "I was a streetwalker in Venice."

Martinis, my girl, are deceiving: Take two at the very most.
Take three and you're under the table.
Take four and you're under the host.

*"I'll have you know I'm not
<u>that</u> kind of a girl."*

In the Unabashed Dictionary we're compiling, the word *pajamas* is defined as an item of clothing usually placed next to the bed in case of fire.

A very plain nurse was telling a voluptuous co-worker about the sailor who was a patient in Ward 10. "He's tattooed," she confided (and her voice dropped low), "in a very *intimate* place!"

"You mean——" gasped the beautiful nurse.

"Yes! Isn't that odd? There's actually a *word* tattooed there. The word 'swan'."

"This I've got to see," exclaimed the voluptuous one, and she hurried off to Ward 10. Half-an-hour later, she returned. "You were right," she said, "he *is* tattooed there. But you were wrong about the word. It's 'Saskatchewan'!"

A technique perfected by a playboy friend of ours is so unique it deserves telling.

Quite recently, he had been having difficulty persuading a lovely but stubborn young lady to part with her Victorian moral principles. He tried soft words and soft music; he tried the cave-man approach; he tried strong drink. She resisted all these devices. Finally, one Saturday afternoon, he escorted her to an extremely fashionable furrier where he asked to see a collection of their finest mink coats. From these he permitted the girlfriend to choose one costing a cool 10 grand.

"I assume you will accept my check," said our

friend in a matter-of-fact manner.

The furrier explained that, being Saturday afternoon, the banks were closed and they would be unable to verify his credit until the following Monday. The playboy smiled. "I understand," he said. "Suppose we leave the coat here—I'll drop by Monday and pick it up. Here is my check."

Monday morning when he returned to the store, the furrier said sternly, "I am sorry, sir, but I cannot let you have the mink coat you ordered Saturday. We have called your bank and find that your account will not cover a check of this size."

"Yes, I know that," our friend replied. "I just stopped by to thank you for a wonderful weekend."

Imagine the girl's surprise when she walked into the playboy's apartment and discovered he had no chairs, no tables, no bed, no furniture at all. She was floored!

Did you ever notice what *motel* spells backward?

A women's-wear manufacturer has announced a new brassiere called Embargo. Doesn't make much sense until you give it the old Serutan twist and spell it backward.

It was her wedding night and the sweet young thing was in a romantic haze. "Oh darling," she sighed, "we're married at last. It's all like a wonderful dream!" Her husband didn't answer.

A few moments passed, she sighed again, and said: "I'm afraid I'll awake in a moment and find it isn't true." Still no response from her spouse.

Another pause and another sensuous sigh, then, softly: "I just can't believe that I'm really your wife."

"Damn it," growled her mate, "as soon as I get this shoelace untied you will!"

News item: Arthur Proctor, of this city, was today accused of signing a false name when applying for a marriage license. The new Mrs. Proctor came to his defense, saying, "Arthur didn't mean to do that—it's just that he's become so accustomed to hotel registers."

We've just received the results of a survey conducted to ascertain the various reasons men get out of bed in the middle of the night. According to the report, 2% are motivated by a desire to visit the bathroom and 3% have an urge to raid the refrigerator.

The other 95% get up to go home.

*"You're confusing me, Miss Barlow."*

"What part of the human body," asked the Anatomy professor, "is harder than steel?" Nobody in the class volunteered the information, so he looked in the direction of a sweet coed and asked, "Can you tell me, Miss Riley?"

She blushed a deep scarlet and lowered her eyes, murmuring, "Oh, *please* don't ask me to answer that, Professor!"

Crisply, he said, "The answer is the tissue of the nails. And you, Miss Riley," he added with a sigh, "are an optimist."


A performing octopus could play the piano, the zither and the piccolo, and his trainer wanted him to add the bagpipe to his accomplishments. With this in mind, a bagpipe was placed in the octopus' room and the trainer awaited results.

Hours passed, but no bagpipe music was heard. Since the talented octopus usually learned quickly, the trainer was disturbed. Opening the door the next morning, he asked the octopus, "Have you learned to play that thing yet?"

"*Play it?!*" retorted the octopus. "I've been trying to *lay* it all night!"


Two shapely stenographers were standing on a crowded subway. One asked the other: "That man behind me—is he good-looking?"

"Well," was the answer, "he's young."

The first girl nodded. "*That* I know."

"Oh—I couldn't accept that, Mr. Rainsford!
Why, we hardly know each other!"

A lovely Southern belle we know is such a slow talker that by the time she got through assuring a friend of ours that she wasn't that kind of girl, she was.

While vacationing last summer in the North Woods, a young fellow thought it might be a good idea to write to his girl. He had brought no stationery with him, however, so he had to walk into town for some. Entering the one and only general store, he discovered that the clerk was a young, full-blown farm girl with languorous eyes. "Do you keep stationery?" he asked.

"Well," she giggled, "I do until the last few seconds, and then I just go wild."

After the age of 45, a man's get up and go is likely to have got up and gone.

The storm smashed the great ship to pieces. One small boat of survivors found its way to a nearby island and safety. Realizing that they had been blown off the usual steamship route and would probably be on the island for many months before being rescued, the survivors proceeded to set up satisfactory living arrangements. Since the survivors included six women and one man, these "arrangements" were a little unusual.

It was agreed among them that rather than fight over the lucky fellow, each girl would take her turn, having him entirely to herself one day each week; and that he would have the seventh day to himself.

Being a normal sort of a guy, our friend threw himself into the situation with a great deal of enthusiasm. The first few weeks, he didn't even bother with his day of rest. As time passed, however, he began looking forward to that one day at the end of each week. Eventually, in fact, it was that day that filled his every thought; he longed to be off the island, to hear a masculine voice again, and to sleep, for days, and days, and days.

One morning, a Saturday, with the week almost at an end, he spotted a small raft on the horizon, and on it a figure. He waved frantically as the raft approached the island, and when it was near enough and he realized that the new arrival was a man, he dashed down the hill to the beach. As the man pulled himself out of the water, our friend threw his arms around him and cried: "Man, you've no idea how glad I am to see you!"

"Well, goodness, fellow," swished the new arrival. "I'm gladda see you, too!"

"My God," croaked the weary one, "there go my Sundays!"

The attractive governess, with her small charge in tow, left the park to visit her boyfriend in his hotel room. They embraced warmly and each longed for intimacy, but there seemed to be little they could do with the child watching. Then the governess hit on an idea.

"Bobby," she said to her small charge, "go look out that window and I will give you a dime for every red hat you see."

Delighted with the new game, Bobby ran to the window and stared intently at the passers-by below.

Almost a minute passed before Bobby's voice piped up with, "I see a red hat!"

"That's nice," came the governess' muffled reply.

"There's another one," said the boy a short time later.

"Keep counting," the woman managed to say.

"Oh, governess," Bobby exclaimed suddenly.

"What now?" she asked, breathing heavily.

"I just wanted to tell you that this is going to be the most expensive roll in the hay you've ever had, 'cause here comes a Shriners' Parade!"

A songwriter friend of ours, the same nifty word merchant who comes up with all those jukebox hits, has turned out another catchy one: *I Used to Kiss Her on the Lips, but It's All Over Now.*

A naive father is one who thinks his daughter has been a good girl because she returns from a date with a Gideon Bible in her purse.

"Now am I supposed to be the bird and you
the bee or is it the other way around?"

Then there was the middle-aged businessman who took his spouse to Paris. After traipsing with her from one *maison du couture* to another, he begged for a day off to rest and got it. With the wife gone shopping again, he went to the Ritz Bar and picked up a luscious *Parisienne*. They got on well until the question of money came up. She wanted 50 American dollars; he offered 10. They couldn't get together on the price, so they didn't get together. That evening he escorted his wife to one of the nicer restaurants on the Rue de Rivoli and there he spotted his gorgeous babe of the afternoon seated at a table near the door.

"See, Monsieur?" she said, as they passed her. "Look what you got for your lousy 10 bucks."

It was a large, lavish dinner party and many important dignitaries and members of society were there.

"I suppose I mustn't offer you wine," said the hostess to the guest of honor seated on her right. "Aren't you the chairman of the Temperance League?"

"Oh, no," replied her guest with a smile, "I'm the head of the Anti-Vice League."

"Oh, of course," said the embarrassed hostess, "I knew there was something I shouldn't offer you."

The curvy little coed in the tight-fitting cashmere sweater wiggled up to the professor after class and murmured in a honeyed voice, "I'm afraid I didn't do very well on that quiz today, Professor. But I'll do

*"I didn't want a big wedding, but
she insisted on it."*

anything to pass this course. Just *anything*."

The professor raised an eyebrow. "Anything?"

"Uh-huh," she cooed. "Anything you ask."

"Then study," he said dryly.

Mrs. Culpepper was almost in tears. "Oh, Marie," she said to her maid, "I believe my husband is having an affair with his secretary."

"I don't believe it," snapped Marie. "You're just saying that to make me jealous."

We were enjoying one of the more sensational Italian films the other evening, and during a torrid love scene, we heard a small voice near us in the darkened theater say, "Mommy, is this where he puts the pollen on her?"

Three female members of an exclusive country club walked into the women's shower room and were shocked to see the lower part of a man's anatomy behind the door of one of the shower stalls. "Well!" said one of the ladies, "that certainly isn't *my* husband!" The second one added, "He isn't mine, either."

And the third, the youngest of the three, said, "Hell, he isn't even a member of the club."

"That wife of mine is a liar," said the angry husband to a sympathetic pal seated next to him in the bar.

"How do you know?" the friend asked.

"She didn't come home last night and when I asked her where she'd been, she said she had spent the night with her sister, Shirley."

"So?"

"She's a liar. *I* spent the night with her sister, Shirley."

"My mother," said the sweet young steno, "says there are some things a girl should not do before 20."

"Your mother is right," said the junior exec. "I don't like a large audience either."

The dean at an exclusive girls' college was lecturing her students on sexual morality.

"In moments of temptation," said the speaker to the class, "ask yourself just one question: Is an hour of pleasure worth a lifetime of shame?"

A sweet young thing in the back of the room rose to ask a question of her own: "How do you make it last an hour?"

A true music lover has been defined as a man who puts his ear to the keyhole when he hears a girl singing in the tub.

The angry woman's voice made the hotel manager wince. "I'm up here in room 1510," she ranted over the phone, "and I want you to know there is a man walking around in the room across the way with not one stitch of clothes on and his shades are up and it's a shocking way to run a hotel."

"I'll send the house detective up right away, madam," the manager assured her, and motioned for his minion of the law to scoot upstairs and see what the hassle was about.

The detective entered the woman's room, peered across the way, and said, "You're right, madam, the gentleman hasn't any clothes on, but his window sill covers him from the waist down no matter where he is in his room."

"Indeed?" yelped the lady. "Stand on the bed! Stand on the bed!"

We know of an overweight playboy who is unhappy about losing 105 pounds last month. She was a beautiful blonde.

He drank with curvy Mabel,
The pace was fast and furious.
He slid beneath the table—
Not drunk, but merely curious.

One of our favorite bartenders told us about a very proper Englishman who came into his place a couple of weeks ago. The fellow sat down at the bar, but didn't order. The bartender, an unusually friendly guy, asked him if he couldn't fix him a drink, on the house.

The Englishman shook his head. "Tried liquor once," he said. "Didn't like it."

The bartender then offered the Englishman a cigarette.

"No, thank you," he said. "Tried tobacco once. Didn't like it."

Still trying to be friendly, the bartender asked the Englishman if he would like to join a couple of friends seated at the bar in a few hands of poker.

The Englishman shook his head. "Tried gambling once. Didn't like it. I wouldn't be sitting in this place at all, but I promised my son I would meet him here."

"I see," said the bartender. "Your only child, I assume."

*"And what do you consider the most important leg of your trip, sir?"*

Rationing, we're told, is pretty much a thing of the past in Great Britain now. But when the austerity program was in full swing, eggs were very hard to get. One store received its allotment and put a sign in the window, announcing: SALE OF EGGS RESTRICTED TO EXPECTANT MOTHERS.

"Put a dozen eggs under the counter for me," requested one young lady. "I'll call for them in the morning."

An attractive young thing met her maiden aunt downtown for lunch one afternoon and during the meal, the older woman asked her niece to deposit a paycheck for her at the bank where the girl worked. On her way back from lunch, the girl was accosted by a purse snatcher.

"Help, help," she screamed at a passing cop. "That man has taken my aunt's pay—he's taken my aunt's pay!"

"OK, lady," said the cop. "Cut out the pig latin and tell me exactly what happened."

Friend Bob Willoughby finally took his long-dreamed-of trip to La Belle France. When he returned, after a two-month visit, we asked him about it.

"Wonderful," he sighed, "especially Paris. My only regret is that I couldn't have made the trip 20 years ago."

"When Paris was really Paris, eh?" we said.

"No," said Bob, a little sadly. "When Willoughby was really Willoughby."


Verily, a man never knows whether he likes bathing beauties until he has bathed one.


Two young men seated in a restaurant were watching a customer busily disposing of a plate of oysters on the half-shell. One of the young men remarked to his friend: "Did you ever hear that business about raw oysters being good for a man's virility?"

"Yes, why?" the friend replied.

"Well, take it from me, that's a lot of foolishness. I ate a dozen of them the other night and only nine worked."


"If I'm not in bed by 10 o'clock," said one female bar-fly to the other, "I'm going home."


One evening at dinner the small boy asked how he had been brought into the world. His father, a rather strait-laced gentleman, tried to dismiss the question with a reference to the stork. Unsatisfied, the youngster asked where the father had come from.

"The stork brought me, too, son," the father replied.

The boy sat quietly for a few moments. Then: "What about Grandfather?" he asked.

"Yes, the stork brought your Grandfather, too," the father snapped, about to lose patience with his son for posing questions that were obviously none of a small boy's business.

"Gee, Dad," the child exclaimed, "do you mean this family has gone through three generations without any sexual intercourse?"


"Men seldom make passes
At girls who wear glasses,"
So Dorothy Parker has said.
She said it quite rightly,
They're very unsightly,
But no one wears glasses to bed.


The svelte young secretary was dissatisfied with her job and so walked into her boss' office one morning and announced that she had found a new position.

"Excellent," the boss exclaimed. "We must try it at once!"


A sweet young thing of our acquaintance decided that

*"Sa-a-ay! This looks like a pretty exciting place!"*

she would rather be a young man's slave than an old man's darling, because she couldn't stand the idea of old age creeping up on her.

**S**hed a tear for the unfortunate shoe salesman, with a lisp, who got slapped when he asked an adequately proportioned female customer to sit down while he "looked up her thize."

**D**emonstrating once again the importance of the lowly comma, this telegram was sent from a wife to her husband: "NOT GETTING ANY, BETTER COME HOME AT ONCE."

**A** svelte redhead was driving her Jag cross-country last summer. The trip was a hot and dusty one and when she spotted a small pool in a little glade not far off the road, she decided to stop for a swim. She slipped out of her clothes and plunged in, and had been enjoying the cool water a few minutes, when she became aware of two farmers watching her from behind some bushes. Her clothes were at the other side of the pool, but there was an old washtub stuck in the sand near her, and holding that in front of her, she marched out of the water toward them.

"Don't you two old fools have anything better to do?" she snapped. "Do you know what I think?!"

"Yes, ma'am," drawled the taller of the two men, "you think that there washtub has a bottom in it."

The golfer confidently eyed the next hole and remarked to his caddy: "This should be good for a long drive and a putt." His swing, however, hit the sod and pushed the ball only a few feet.

"Now," said the caddy, "for a hell of a putt."

A world-traveling friend who has just returned from Tibet informs us that a coolie is a quickie in the snow.

The outraged husband discovered his wife in bed with another man.

"What is the meaning of this?" he demanded. "Who is this fellow?"

"That seems like a fair question," said the wife, rolling over. "What *is* your name?"

A streetwalking acquaintance of ours has a new slogan that's certain to revolutionize her trade: "It's a business to do pleasure with you."

Engineers are continually surprised to find that girls with the most streamlined shapes offer the most resistance.

The stranger walked up to a Las Vegas dice table and laid down a $1000 bet. He shook the dice, but as he threw them a third cube fell unexpectedly from his sleeve. The house operator was unruffled. He handed back two of the dice and pocketed the third, saying, "OK, roll again. Your point is 15."

On a windy street corner, a shapely miss held tightly to her hat with both hands while her skirt billowed higher and higher about her legs. In response to the amused glances of two masculine passers-by, she explained with refreshing candor: "What you are looking at is 23 years old, gentlemen; what I'm hanging onto is brand new."

The police were investigating the mysterious death of

a prominent businessman who had jumped from a window of his 11th-story office. His voluptuous private secretary could offer no explanation for the action, but said that her boss had been acting peculiarly ever since she started working for him a month ago.

"After my very first week on the job," she said, "I received a $20 raise. At the end of the second week, he called me into his private office, gave me a lovely black nightie, five pairs of nylon stockings, and said, 'These are for a beautiful, efficient secretary.'

"At the end of the third week, he gave me a gorgeous mink stole. Then, this afternoon he called me into his private office again, presented me with this fabulous diamond bracelet, and asked me if I would consider making love to him and what it would cost.

"I told him I would and because he had been so nice to me, he could have it for five dollars, although I was charging all the other boys in the office $10. That's when he jumped out the window."

In a recent discussion on world affairs, a friend observed the difference between war and peace is there has never been a good war.

The new inmate at the mental hospital announced in a loud voice that he was the famous British naval hero, Lord Nelson. This was particularly interesting, because the institution already had a "Lord Nelson." The head psychiatrist, after due consideration, decided to put the two men in the same room, feeling that the

"Uh—didn't you forget to take your stetho-
scope with you under the covers, doctor?"

similarity of their delusions might prompt an adjustment in each that would help in curing them. It was a calculated risk, of course, for the men might react violently to one another, but they were introduced and then left alone and no disturbance was heard from the room that night.

The next morning, the doctor had a talk with his new patient and was more than pleasantly surprised when he was told: "Doctor, I've been suffering from a delusion. I know now that I am *not* Lord Nelson."

"That's wonderful," said the doctor.

"Yes," said the patient, smiling demurely, "I'm Lady Hamilton."

An old man, walking down the street, saw a small boy sitting on the curb crying. He stopped and asked, "Little boy, why are you crying?"

The little boy said, "I'm crying because I can't do what the big boys do." So the old man sat down alongside of him and cried, too.

Three decrepit, gray-haired gentlemen were seated together in the park discussing their personal philosophies for achieving a ripe old age.

"I'm 86," said the first, "and I wouldn't be here today if I hadn't scorned tobacco and alcohol in every form, avoided late hours and the sinful enticements of the opposite sex."

"I owe my 93 years to a strict diet of blackstrap molasses, wheat-germ bread and mother's milk," said

"*We'll never be able to use this scene,
but what the hell, keep shooting!*"

the second old man.

"When I was 18," the third man said, "my father told me that if I wanted to enjoy life as much as he had, I should smoke black cigars, drink nothing but hard liquor, and carouse with a different woman every night. And that's exactly what I've done."

"Incredible," said the first old man.

"Amazing," said the second, for their friend was obviously the grayest, most elderly appearing of the three. "Just how old are you?"

"Twenty-two."

You've undoubtedly heard about the number of magazines required to fill a baby carriage: a PLAYBOY, a *Mademoiselle*, a few *Liberties* and *Time*.

You might say that a girl has reached the awkward age when she is too old to count on her fingers and too young to count on her legs.

Canned and frozen juices are becoming more and more popular, but most men still prefer to squeeze their own tomatoes.

Recent statistics indicate that 70% of the women with breast cancer attribute it to men who smoke.

A doctor and his wife were out walking when a buxom

blonde in tight-fitting sweater and skirt nodded hello from a nearby doorway.

"And who was that?" questioned the wife.

"Oh, just a young woman I know professionally," said the doctor, reddening visibly.

"I'm sure of that," said the wife, "but your profession or hers?"

A master plumber was explaining some of the finer points of job etiquette to his apprentice. "Working in other people's homes," he said, "you're bound to run into some embarrassing situations, but you can usually get out of them by using a little tact. Now take the other day as an example: I entered a bathroom to do some work and found a young lady taking a bath. I backed out right away, saying, 'Excuse me, sir.' That way, the lady thought I hadn't gotten a good look at her and she wasn't embarrassed."

The following afternoon the apprentice staggered into the office, his clothes torn, eyes blackened, nose bloodied.

"What happened?" exclaimed the boss.

"You and your tact," cried the apprentice. "I got a call to fix a leaky faucet in the bridal suite of the Plaza Hotel and I was halfway across the bedroom before I realized there was a couple making love in the bed. The husband started to swear at me, so right away I remembered what you'd said, and tipped my hat and said, 'Oh, excuse me, gentlemen.' "

Lord Chesterfield made this rather wry commentary on *la grande passion*: (1) The enjoyment is quite temporary. (2) The cost is quite exorbitant. (3) And the position is simply ridiculous.

The attractive young lady was worried about her sailor boyfriend, away at sea, and complained to her doctor that she couldn't sleep at night. She requested some sleeping tablets, but the doctor suggested she try a psychological technique before resorting to drugs. "Since counting sheep and the other more usual methods have failed," he said, "try repeating this little ritual each night when you retire: 'Toes go to sleep, feet go to sleep, ankles go to sleep, legs go to sleep, thighs go to sleep,' and so on, all the way to the top of your head. Concentrate on each separate part of your body as you direct it to sleep, and before you know it, you'll be in dreamland."

The young lady was dubious, but that very night, after turning out the light and getting into bed, she

"And you were wrong, Mother . . . I liked it."

tried the doctor's suggestion.

"Toes go to sleep," she began. "Feet go to sleep, ankles go to sleep, legs go to sleep, thighs go to sleep . . ."

Suddenly the door to her apartment burst open and in walked her sailor boyfriend.

"Everybody up," she exclaimed, *"everybody up!"*

On an isolated stretch of beach near Cannes, a beautiful French girl threw herself into the sea and drowned despite a young man's attempts to save her. The man dragged the half-nude body ashore and left it on the sand while he went to notify the authorities. Upon his return, he was horrified to see a man making love to the corpse.

*"Monsieur, Monsieur,"* he shouted, "that woman is dead, that woman is dead!"

*"Sacré bleu,"* exclaimed the man, springing up. "I thought she was an American girl."

A friend of ours sat down next to another passenger on a train recently and couldn't help overhearing his conversation out the window with a man standing on the station platform.

"Thanks for putting me up while I was here, Sam," said the passenger.

"Glad to do it," said the other man.

"Thanks for the food and the drinks—everything was wonderful."

"It was a pleasure," said the man.

"I could _swear_ I smell burning rubber!"

"And thank your wife, Sam—she was great," said the passenger, as the train began pulling out. "I really enjoyed sleeping with her."

Our friend was rather taken aback by this exchange and he turned to his fellow passenger and said: "Pardon me, sir, but I couldn't help overhearing your conversation. Did I understand you to say that you enjoyed sleeping with your friend's wife?"

"Well," said the fellow passenger, "I didn't *really* enjoy it. But Sam is a hell of a nice guy."

**"Y**ou want to know why I've come home half loaded?" said the soused spouse. "Because I ran out of money, that's why."

**T**he movie producer traveled all the way to Europe, but had to return to Hollywood disappointed. He contacted the beautiful Italian actress he'd been seeking, all right, but, unfortunately, she refused to come across.

The wife of a friend of ours purchased a rather large grandfather clock at an auction and then sent her unhappy husband to pay for it and carry the damn thing home. To make matters worse, the husband had been to a formal dinner earlier in the evening and was still wearing his full-dress suit. He was having some difficulty with the unwieldy mechanism even before he met the drunk staggering in the opposite direction. They collided and the husband fell backward to the sidewalk, the clock on top of him.

"Why in blazes don't you watch where you're going?!" the angry husband demanded.

The drunk shook his head dazedly, looked at the man in the full-dress suit and at the grandfather clock that lay across him.

"Why don't you wear a wrish watch like everybody elsh," he inquired.

An attractive young lady was having difficulty keeping her skirt down about her shapely legs while awaiting a bus on a windy street corner. She was aware of a man watching her discomfort with considerable interest and she addressed him in an irritated voice: "It is obvious, sir, that you are no gentleman."

With appreciation in his voice, the man replied, "It's obvious that you're not either."

We occasionally get our kicks in a place where the music is so bad that when a waiter drops a tray everybody gets up and starts dancing.

"All right, lady," said the bill collector, "how about the next installment on that couch?"

The lady shrugged. "Better than having to give you money, I guess."

One of our friends has a real problem. He received a note through the mail advising him, "If you don't stop making love to my wife, I'll kill you." The trouble is, the note wasn't signed.

Lord Duffingham returned from his grouse shooting somewhat earlier than usual and found Lady Duffingham in a rather compromising situation with his best friend, Sir Archibald Carpley. Lord Duffingham stood stiffly in the bedroom doorway and loudly berated his wife for her infidelity. With thunder in his voice, he reminded her that he had taken her from a miserable existence in the London slums, given her a fine home, provided her with servants, expensive clothes and jewels.

As Lady Duffingham was by this time crying inconsolably, his Lordship turned his wrath on his supposed friend: "And as for you, Carpley—you might at least stop while I'm talking!"

Anna sat on an anthill at a picnic with most unfortunate results. She asked her sister to send a telegram to their mother and tell her what happened. The sister, faced with the problem of telling the tale in a way acceptable to Western Union and having only enough

*"When you come right down to it, Mr. Bigelow
—casting for TV is just like for movies."*

money for a six-word wire, came up with this message:
"ANACIN HOSPITAL ADAMANT BITTER ASININE PLACES."


**A** rather inebriated fellow on a bus was tearing up a newspaper into tiny pieces and throwing them out the window.

"Excuse me," said the woman sitting next to him, "but would you mind explaining why you're tearing up that paper and throwing the pieces out the window?"

"It scares away the elephants," said the drunk.

"I don't see any elephants," said the woman, smiling.

"Effective, isn't it?" said the drunk.


**T**he young man had invited his fiancée to meet his parents over cocktails at the Plaza. After his family had departed, the girl wanted to know whether she had made the proper impression on them.

"I'm sorry to have to tell you this, dearest," the fellow said, "but while you were in the ladies' room, my mother told me that she considered you rather uncouth."

"Did you tell them that I attended Bennington *and* Mt. Holyoke?" she asked in surprise.

"Yes, dearest."

"Did you remind them that my family enjoys a particularly high standing in Bar Harbor?"

"Yes, I did."

"And I hope you told them of my considerable in-

"*Every time I get a chest cold, it seems to last forever.*"

terest in the arts."

"Of course," said the young man.

"Then what's this 'uncouth' crap all about?" she asked.

In olden days, man's greatest fear was that a woman would take it to heart; today, his greatest fear is that a woman will take it to court.

"Darling, I have a confession to make," said the shy young bride at their first breakfast together. "It isn't a big thing, but I feel I should have told you before. I suffer from asthma."

"Thank heavens," said the groom, smiling. "Last night I thought you were hissing me."

Several gentlemen at the Biltmore Bar were discussing their troubles. Hard-Luck Harry topped them all when he dejectedly explained that he had a wife, a secretary, and a note from the bank—all overdue.

The switchboard operator in a swank New York hotel received a call at a little past two in the morning from a somewhat inebriated man who wanted to know what time the hotel bar opened.

"At nine A.M., sir," she replied.

At 3:30 A.M. the phone rang again and the same man, this time obviously feeling no pain, asked the same question.

"Not until nine A.M.," she said a second time.

At 5:15 A.M. the switchboard operator received still another call from the same guy, now completely stoned. Once again he asked the same question.

More than a little irritated, she snapped, "I told you, sir, you'll have to wait until nine A.M. to get in the bar."

"*Get in*, hell," croaked the drunk, "I want to get *out* of the damned place!"

We just heard about the street cleaner who got fired because he couldn't keep his mind in the gutter.

The very swank men's club had for years forbidden the presence of women in any of its stately rooms. One night a dignified member walked in and was shocked to discover a covey of chirruping ladies gathered in the very center of the study.

"What is the meaning of this?" he demanded of the club manager.

"We've decided to let members bring their wives in for dinner one evening a month," was the reply.

"But that's unfair," complained the disgruntled fellow. "I'm not married. Could I bring my girlfriend?"

The manager thought for a moment, and then replied slowly, "I think it might be all right . . . provided she's the wife of a member."


Breathes there a man with soul so dead,
Who's never to his playmate said:
"To hell with breakfast,
Come back to bed!"


The new patient was airing his woes to an understanding doctor: "After the first, I'm tired, Doc. After the second, my chest aches and I start getting pains in my legs. After the third, I feel like fainting and it takes half-an-hour for my heart and respiration to return to normal."

"Why don't you quit after the first?" inquired the doctor.

"How can I do that, Doc?" the patient asked. "I live on the third."

*"Look, Ginger—George and I are engaged!"*

"I told my boyfriend I didn't want to see him anymore," said the pony-tailed model to her friend, over lunch.

"What did he say?" the friend asked.

"Nothing. He just pulled the covers over his head."

An optimist is a man who looks forward to marriage. A pessimist is a married optimist.

"I really don't know what you see in him, my dear," said the fresh young thing to her lunch companion. "He's just an everyday sort of man."

"Gee," was the response, "what more could a girl ask for?"

Two buddies had been out drinking for hours when their money finally ran out.

"I have an idea," croaked Al. "Lesh go over to my housh and borrow shum money from my wife."

The two of them reeled into Al's living room, snapped on the light, and, lo and behold, there was Al's wife making love on the sofa to another man. This state of affairs considerably unnerved Al's friend but didn't seem to affect the husband. "Shay, dear, you have any money for your ever-lovin' hushban'?" he asked. "Yes, yes," she snapped, "take my purse from the mantel, and, for Pete's sake, turn off those lights." Outside they examined the purse, and Al proudly announced, "There's enough here for a pint

"The devil of it is, with Mt. Everest out of the way, there's nothing left to climb."

for you and a pint for me. Pretty good, eh, old buddy?" "But, Al," protested his friend somewhat sobered by the spectacle he'd just witnessed, "what about that fellow back there with your wife?" "The hell with him," replied Al. "Let him buy his own pint."

We approve of this tactful variation on the age-old delicate question: One asks his date for the evening if she'd like to join him for breakfast. Receiving an affirmative reply, he then asks, "Shall I call you or nudge you?"

The jealous husband returned home from a business trip a day early and discovering a strange coat in the front closet, stormed into the living room with the accusation that there was another man in the apartment.

"Where is he?" the husband demanded, as he stalked from room to room, searching.

"You're mistaken, dear," the wife insisted. "That coat must have been left by one of your friends the last time you threw a poker party. Since you've been gone, I haven't even *looked* at another man."

The husband searched through the entire apartment and, finding no one, decided his wife must be telling the truth. Apologizing for his unwarranted display of temper, he then went to the bathroom to wash up. He was running water in the basin, when he noticed that the shower curtain was pulled closed. Rather peculiar, he thought. He ripped the curtain open and—sure enough—there was a strange man. But before the astounded husband could utter a word, the man jerked the curtain closed again, saying, "Please! I haven't finished voting yet."

**O**ur Research Department has come up with the significant statistic that the average number of times a girl says no to temptation is once weakly.

**T**he baby-faced, brown-eyed secretary phoned her mother to inform her: "I'll be late again for dinner tonight, Mom. I made a mistake last night and the boss wants me to do it over again."

**"I** was in a phone booth talking to my girl, Your Honor," said the defendant, "and this cop came up, opened the door, grabbed me by the coat and dragged me out."

"What did you do?" the judge asked.

"I didn't do anything, not until he grabbed my girl and dragged her out, too."

**177**

We like the letter of resignation offered by a charming young secretary who was forced to quit her job because of embarrassing circumstances: "Dear Boss," it began, "I'm getting too big for this job. . . ."

A girl's kisses usually leave something to be desired: the rest of her.

"Get this," the husband chuckled. "That ridiculous janitor of ours claims he's made love to every woman in the building except one."

"Hmmmm," said his wife, assuming a thoughtful, faraway expression, "must be that stuck-up Mrs. Frobisher on the fourth floor."

The beautiful young lady strolled through the zoo, and finally stopped in front of the monkey island. Mystified as to the whereabouts of the animals, she queried the keeper, "Where are all the monkeys today?"

"They're back in the cave, Miss, it's the mating season."

"Will they come out if I throw them some peanuts?"

The keeper scratched his head, "I don't know, Miss. Would you?"

A fellow we know is so jaded, he has dropped all the subtle preliminaries usually expected by a girl in favor of the direct approach and we recently overheard the following dialog with a young lady he had just met

178

"I'm afraid, Miss Kipulski, we are
running out of clay."

at a cocktail party.

"I'm a man of few words. Will you or won't you?"

"Your apartment or mine?" the sophisticated miss responded.

"Well," he said in an exasperated tone, "if there's going to be such a lot of discussion about it, let's forget the whole damn thing."


**A** friend of ours gave his favorite playmate a diamond wrist watch and the following night, he reports, he gave her the works.


**T**he farm had been mortgaged, and gladly, to give daughter a college education. Now, driving home from the station after meeting her at the train, farmer Johnson was greatly disturbed when his daughter whispered confidentially, "I have a confession to make, Paw—I ain't a virgin no more."

The old man shook his head sadly. "After all the sacrifices your Maw and I made to give you a good education, you still say 'ain't'!"


**"I**'ve good news for you," said the psychiatrist. "You're a well man. It won't be necessary for you to continue the analysis any longer."

"How wonderful, doctor," said the patient. "I'm so very pleased, I wish there were something special I could do for you in return."

"Oh, that's not necessary. You've paid your bill and

"For heaven's sake, Miriam, what if I had
been someone else?"

that's all that's expected."

"But really, doctor, I'm so elated I could kiss you!"

"No, don't do that. Actually, we shouldn't even be lying here on the couch together."

**T**he visiting American was quite upset by his sudden drop in popularity. During his first two weeks in England, he had been invited everywhere, feted and entertained. Now, quite suddenly, his phone no longer jingled and no invitations crowded his mailbox. Perplexed, he called his friend, Reginald.

"Reggie, you can speak frankly with me, what's happened? I'm being virtually ostracized."

"Well, old boy," Reggie replied, "you'll remember that fox hunt you went on last weekend? Here in England it's customary to cry 'Tally ho!' when you sight the fox—not, I'm afraid, 'There goes the little sonofabitch!'"

**"W**ho," raged the angry employer, "told you that just

because I've kissed you a few times you could loaf around the office and neglect your work?"

"My attorney," cooed his secretary.

**T**he young man relaxed on the bed, enjoying a cigarette; his girlfriend lay beside him, lost in thought.

"Darling," she said unexpectedly, as girls are wont to do, "let's get married."

The young man took a long drag on his cigarette and without turning, said, "Dearest, who would have us?"

**S**he was a gorgeous girl.
And he was a loving male.
He praised her shape in English,
French, Italian, and Braille.

**T**he sweet young thing was shopping for her wedding gown.

"Have you been married before?" asked the salesgirl.

"Why, no—why do you ask?"

"Well, when a girl has been previously married, it's customary to wear lavender rather than white."

"Oh. Well let's see what you have in white with lavender trim."


**F**rom London comes the story of the three professors of literature who, while returning from luncheon, encountered several ladies of pleasure who were patrolling the street en masse. "What might one call such a congregation?" mused the first professor, a Shakespearean specialist: "A flourish of strumpets?"

The second professor, being an authority on the novels of Anthony Trollope, naturally contributed "a chapter of trollops."

But the best description, we think, came from the youngest and least specialized of the professors. He called the ladies "an anthology of pros."


**M**iss Bradshaw, a comely high-school teacher, had saved money for several years and was finally aboard a sleek ocean liner for her long-anticipated trip to Europe. Aboard ship, she wrote:

"Dear Diary: MONDAY. I felt singularly honored this evening. The Captain asked me to dine at his table. TUESDAY. I spent the entire morning on the bridge with the Captain. WEDNESDAY. The Captain made proposals to me unbecoming an officer and a gentleman. THURSDAY. Tonight the captain threat-

*". . . and now for another hour of uninterrupted music."*

ened to sink the ship if I do not give in to his indecent proposals. FRIDAY. This afternoon I saved 1600 lives."

Our Unabashed Dictionary defines an efficient nurse as one who can make a patient without disturbing the bed.

The best way to approach a woman with a past is with a present.

Girls who look good in the best places usually get taken there.

Women who insist on wearing the pants frequently discover that it is other women who are wearing the chinchilla.

Bill's sister was one of the most popular girls in Manhattan. She had more boyfriends than she knew what to do with and she never wanted for a thing. Bill was an impecunious musician, always in debt and constantly asking his sister for spending money.

"I don't understand you, Bill," she said in obvious annoyance one afternoon when he had tried to put the bite on her for a 10 spot. "I don't have any trouble saving money, so why should you?"

"Sure, sure," he said, "but you've got money coming in all the time from the very thing that's keeping me broke."

"Careful . . . my husband is
having me watched."

**"F**or 20 long and wonderful years," mused the gentleman at the bar, "my wife and I were deliriously happy."

"Then what happened?" asked the bartender.

"We met."

**O**ur Unabashed Dictionary defines a *metallurgist* as a man who can look at a platinum blonde and tell whether she is virgin metal or a common ore.

**T**he high-priced lawyer was sitting in his office when his secretary announced the arrival of a new client: a very sexy dish.

"I wish to divorce my husband," said the dish.

"On what grounds?" the lawyer asked.

"Infidelity," came the reply. "I don't think my husband has been faithful to me."

"What makes you think that?"

"Well," said the dame, "I don't think he's the father of my child."

"Love of my life," said the enraptured husband, "your beauty is such that it should be captured in the nude by the finest sculptor in the world."

Two gentlemen passing by the hotel room happened to overhear the conversation, paused for a moment, then rapped on the door.

"Who's there?" asked the husband.

"Two sculptors from New York," came the answer.

We've just heard about the old maid who sued a Miami Beach hotel for cruelty. Seems they gave her a room between two honeymooning couples.

If Dorothy Parker will forgive us, it is our observation that men often make passes at girls who drain glasses.

The long-shanked, ash-blonde Hollywood starlet was grappling with the producer in his Laurel Canyon home for a full half-hour. Finally, with a supreme effort, she picked herself up off the couch, straightened her stockings, brushed the hair off her forehead, looked him straight in the eye and said, "Flirt."

"Tsk, tsk," said the unhappy executive, "I had to fire my new secretary today."

"How come?" asked the friend. "No experience?"

"None whatever," the exec replied. "I told her to sit down for some dictation and she looked around for a chair."

"You beast. You animal," cried the young thing. "I'm going back to Mother."

"Never mind," said the guy. "I'll go back to my wife."

A friend of ours who travels by plane a good deal says that his pet peeve is the good-looking airline stewardess who straps him in his seat and then asks, "Is there anything you'd like?"

Janice, the cute upstairs maid in the Johnson household, came to her mistress with a sad story to tell. Janice, it seemed, was going to have a baby—out of wedlock—and she would have to quit. Mrs. Johnson, though stunned, came back with a game offer, for good servants are hard to find, and Janice was good.

"You'll do no such thing, my dear," she said. "You'll have your child here and we'll adopt it and raise it as our own." And so it was arranged, and everybody was happy.

But the following year, it was the same story. Once again Mrs. Johnson insisted that the family adopt the child and Janice stay on. The third year was a repeat performance.

When Janice came to her for the fourth time, Mrs. Johnson shook her head from side to side. "Janice, Janice," she said, "whatever are we to do with you?"

"There's nothing to be done, madam," said Janice. "This time I'm truly leaving. I refuse to work for such a large family."

*". . . We did <u>what</u> along with Mitch last night?!"*

"Hey, wise guy," complained the delightful dish, "what's the big idea? You promised you'd take me to Florida!"

"I said nothing of the sort," insisted her gentleman friend. "I merely commented that I was going to Tampa with you."

The incident took place on the boat deck of the S.S. United States the first day at sea. A well-stacked young morsel, out for a stroll, bumped into an officer as both rounded a corner. They drew back, apologized, stepped forward, and bumped again. A third try produced the same results. This time the officer courteously tipped his cap and said, "Just once more, miss—and then I really must go."